GAGAKU

GAGAKU
Court Music and Dance

by Masataro Togi

translated by Don Kenny

with an introduction by
William P. Malm

A WEATHERHILL BOOK

WALKER/WEATHERHILL, *New York & Tokyo*
IN COLLABORATION WITH TANKOSHA, KYOTO

This book was originally published in Japanese
by Tankosha, under the title *Gagaku*.

FIRST EDITION, 1971

Jointly published by John Weatherhill, Inc., of New York and Tokyo, and Tankosha
of Kyoto / Distributed in the Far East by JOHN WEATHERHILL, INC., 7-6-13 Roppongi,
Minato-ku, Tokyo 106, and in the United States by WALKER AND COMPANY, 720
Fifth Avenue, New York, N.Y. 10019 / Copyright © 1968, 1971, by Tankosha.
Printed in Japan

LCC CARD NO. 77-139689
ISBN 0-8027-2445-0

Table of Contents

v

GAGAKU

The Special Characteristics
of Gagaku

by William P. Malm

MY FIRST CONTACT with Gagaku was in 1955 when I attended
an outdoor concert given in the outer grounds of the Imperial
Palace in Tokyo. The costumed musicians played diligently
while amateur photographers crawled all over the edges of the
platform, shouting advice to one another about speeds, aper-
tures, and angles for good shots. I recall in particular one
Japanese photographer who squatted close to a flute player
and proceeded to "shoot" him like some kind of exotic animal.
The flute player continued to perform, but his eyes bored into
the camera with a hate and resentment which would have
made a far more meaningful and powerful picture if the photographer had only been sensitive enough to realize it.

Not long after, I heard Gagaku in Tokyo's Hibiya Hall in
a public concert. On this occasion news and TV cameramen
broke into each piece with huge floodlights that swept alternately into the eyes of the performers and the audience as
noisy movie cameras whirled out their few feet of "interesting"
film.

Finally, I had an invitation to hear Gagaku in its special

performance hall in the Imperial Palace compound. Foreigners equaled or surpassed in number the Japanese in attendance as the subtle sounds filled the austere hall. The click of a camera and the occasional indiscreet flash of a bulb broke the spell for only brief moments, but they caused me to reflect upon this most special musical tradition and its place in the modern world. After the concert my meditations were further stimulated by the sight of a nearby orchestral rehearsal room where, I was told, these same musicians had to practice Western-style music in order to entertain at imperial receptions of a less formal nature.

In 1955 the click of the camera and the flow of Western-style harmonies were certainly more a part of the modern Japanese tradition than Gagaku, and yet Gagaku was still surviving. At that time one could say that it seemed to be continued as a museum piece and as a model for photographers. Since that time, however, we have seen a more genuine revival of interest in Gagaku. This is evidenced by such things as an international tour by the imperial troupe, an impressive set of new recordings, an increase in both foreign and Japanese publications concerning Gagaku, and the creation of new ensembles, including one at the Tokyo University of Fine Arts as well as one in the United States. Perhaps as we discuss the characteristics of Gagaku we can discover some of the reasons why this tradition has survived and, to a certain extent, even flourished in the modern, transistor-oriented world of Japan.

The distinctive nature of Gagaku can be seen from many viewpoints, but we will discuss only three of them here: the special qualities of Gagaku as history, interesting aspects of the instruments of Gagaku, and the sounds of Gagaku as they relate to the modern aesthetic taste.

Elsewhere in this book you can read in detail the fascinating history of Gagaku and its many connections with the ancient Orient. Thanks to the diligence of such Japanese scholars as Hayashi Kenzo,* Kishibe Shigeo, and Tanabe Hisao, as well as Eta Harich-Schneider, Hans Eckert, and Robert Garfias in the West, we know in considerable detail of the survivals of ancient Indian, Southeast Asian, Chinese, Manchurian, and Korean traditions in the music and dance of the Nara (710–84) and Heian (794–1185) Japanese courts. Certainly this is one of the first fascinations of Japanese Gagaku and its continental companion the Korean Aak, for they are almost the only living sources through which we can catch a glimpse of the musical splendors of Asia during the brilliant seventh, eighth, and ninth centuries. One can imagine the joy there would be in the West if musicologists had such a direct channel to the musical traditions of medieval Europe. Of course no one believes that the Gagaku played today is a precise copy of its original sound. Centuries of alternate support and neglect, as well as the consolidation of styles in the Nara and Heian periods and the forcible joining of long-separated schools in the Meiji era (1868–1912), have obviously caused the repertoire and the style of playing to change. In addition, the very age of Gagaku lends to it that kind of aura that makes most musicians play old music more slowly than necessary. Nevertheless, one cannot . escape the fact that Gagaku has managed to survive in a form that must make it the oldest continuous orchestral tradition in the world.

*All Japanese personal names in this book are given in Japanese order: surname first, given name last.

When one views the overall history of ancient Asia, Japan can often be seen as a kind of cultural *cul-de-sac*. The traditions of the ancient Near East and India came across the trade routes to China and from there were passed over the sea to Japan. They could go no farther. Asian culture, so to speak, piled up in Japan like water behind a dam. The greatest flow of materials came in the eighth century during the height of the Chinese T'ang dynasty. By the ninth century the Chinese court was in such turmoil that Japan stopped sending official envoys. This move effectively isolated the Gagaku tradition from its continental roots. Cut off from further foreign influence, the many foreign and Japanese styles of music surviving in Gagaku were eventually consolidated into the two basic categories used today: Togaku (music deriving from China and Southeast Asia) and Komagaku (music deriving from Korea). After some further Heian-period adjustments the repertoire remained rather set.

Perhaps even then many things might not have survived if the troops of Kublai Khan had managed to prevail on that fateful day in 1281 when they attempted to invade Japan. To understand the cultural importance of this event, we may look at what happened to those continental Asian centers which were unable to resist Mongol intrusions. The desert centers of Turfan, Kucha, and Khotan were reduced to dust by assorted invaders, while in mighty China itself the basic mode of living altered considerably when the Mongol dynasty began. In Chinese music such changes included the adoption of the foreign fiddle (*hu ch'in*), cymbals, new oboes (*sona*), and Central Asian plucked lutes, the most important of which remains today in the form of the *san hsien*. Some of these instruments filtered on to Japan and there evolved local forms such as the three-stringed, banjolike *shamisen* and the *kokyu,* a three-stringed violin. These later changes, however, affected chiefly the music of the general Japanese populace, particularly the *chonin* (townsmen). Gagaku remained basically unaffected.

Continuing the analogy made earlier, one could say that the old stream of Asian culture stopped and a new river appeared from a new source, flowing in a different direction. Since Gagaku had been the final point in the old stream bed, there remained at this terminus a quiet, isolated pool. Fresh waters flowed elsewhere while this pool of old culture was left to mellow and to acquire that special charm so valued in Asia: the charm of something which has acquired a patina of age and neglect without losing its grace and beauty. Thus it is that history has placed Gagaku in its special niche.

This special sense of history brings to mind an overwhelming experience I had while visiting the ruins of Angkor Vat in Cambodia. As I walked along the miles of delicate bas-relief, now surrounded by jungle, I caught endless insights into the life and death of the Khmer civilization. The most powerful moment of that visit occurred while I was standing before a relief on the side of the Bayan Temple. Here I saw acrobats, wrestlers, and musicians entertaining in a manner very much like that which one sees depicted on the weapons and instruments found in the Shoso-in treasure house at Nara. At one point in this relief the figures become incomplete, and eventually one sees only the preliminary outlines of the next person to be carved. As I stood there in the steaming heat of a Cambodian summer, I realized that I was looking at the precise moment of the end of a civilization. It was at this point, centuries ago, that the artist dropped his chisel, never to return. The fate of civilizations has never been more poignantly demonstrated for me than at that moment. How many magnificent civilizations of Asia are known to us today only in the form of ruins, documents, or perhaps only in legends? Looking again at Gagaku in this context, one realizes that, thanks to its relative isolation, it holds a unique attraction. Though some may consider it a stagnant tradition, it must be realized that the very removal of Gagaku from the mainstream of Japanese musical life has allowed it to preserve musical history for us in a way unknown even in the rest of Asia. I wonder if there ever was such a history-laden musical tradition anywhere else in the world.

We have emphasized the unique position of Gagaku in Pan-Asiatic history, but we must not overlook its special contributions to the study of Japanese history as well. Among the forms of Gagaku, *kagura* preserves Shinto rituals which had their origins in the very earliest Japanese imperial traditions. The *azuma asobi* and *kume uta* of the Nara period, also preserved in Gagaku, employ the basic symbols of Shinto and contain references to the basic legends in Japan's two oldest chronicles, the *Kojiki* and the *Nihon Shoki*. *Kagura* was codified in the Heian period, and an annual imperial performance has been held in an unbroken tradition from the eleventh century until today. In this we have perhaps the oldest continuous form of music which is of Japanese as against foreign origin.

The musical forms *roei* and *saibara* also reflect for us indigenous Japanese courtly tastes in the Heian period. Thus we can add to our list of Gagaku's special qualities its ability to evoke Japan's most brilliant courtly period. The Heian-period writings of Lady Murasaki and Sei Shonagon are filled with references to music, some of which belonged to the types surviving in Gagaku today. Of course, much has been lost. The solo instrumental traditions referred to in Lady Murasaki's novel *The Tale of*

Genji disappeared with the rise of more plebeian forms. The last singer of the once popular *imayo* songs passed away in the late nineteenth century, leaving only the tradition of singing a text to the tune of the Gagaku piece *Etenraku* as a reminder of the style of the *imayo* form.

While Gagaku was certainly out of the mainstream of Japanese musical development from the Muromachi period (1338–1573) through the Edo period (1603–1868), it did have a special importance in the Meiji era. Since the era began with the restoration of the emperor as head of state, things which had a traditional connection with the emperor—for example, Gagaku—enjoyed a new emphasis. The other driving motive of the Meiji era, modernization, also affected the fate of the Gagaku musicians. These men, being the only musicians directly connected with the imperial household, were chosen to be some of the first performers of Western music. Along with the newly formed military bands, the Gagaku ensemble gained great prestige through its ability to play marches and polkas, and the musicians were in great demand as teachers and performers of Western music as well as of Gagaku. Because of their close connections with the power structure of the early Meiji era, the Gagaku musicians were also involved in the creation of the national anthem and of songs for use in the newly formed public-school music system. While most of the Gagaku-oriented school songs have not survived, the national anthem remains, and, as we have noted, the Gagaku musicians still play Western music. But the main practitioners of Western music in Japan are found elsewhere today, and the special value of the court musicians lies in their skill at retaining the traditional repertoire.

Nevertheless, as we view the special historical values of Gagaku, we must not overlook the unique role that its musicians played in the formation of a Western tradition in Japan. This uniqueness is all the more powerful when one realizes that historically Gagaku musicians were vehicles for the introduction of the two foreign traditions of greatest importance to Japanese music, which appeared at the two ends of the so-called traditional period of Japanese culture. At one end was Chinese court music in the Nara period, and at the other was Western music in the Meiji era. Gagaku musicians were not involved in the equally important changes that occurred in theater music in the fourteenth and sixteenth centuries, nor were they active in the great expansion of plebeian music in the seventeenth century. Still, from the overview of the history of Japanese music presented here, one can see that whenever there was a rise in imperial power Gagaku musicians were capable of taking active roles in the shaping of new musical traditions. It remains to be seen whether, under the present conditions of a constitutional monarchy, Gagaku musicians will be able to influence the course of Japanese music again. Perhaps not, but their past contributions have certainly earned them a place of respect and honor regardless of their future activities.

Before leaving this discussion of the special qualities of Gagaku as history, I should like to point out an interesting analogy which can be made between the origins of Western art music and that of Japan. Both of these types of music seem to have grown out of two kinds of previous traditions. For Western art music, one of these was the basic style and nomenclature of the music of the Catholic church, as exemplified in the so-called Gregorian chant codified in the sixth century. The other base of Western music was the interpretation of the "foreign" music tradition and theory of ancient Greece as it was understood by Roman

1. Bato: *a dance of the left*

2. *Orchestral performance by imperial Gagaku troupe, Tokyo*

3. Nasori: *a dance of the right*

4. Manzairaku: *a dance of the left*

5. Bairo: *a dance of the right*

6. Engiraku: *a dance of the right*

7. *Yamato* mai: *an ancient native Japanese dance*

and Christian scholars. The first base of Japanese art music was the style and musical nomenclature of Buddhist chant, as exemplified by *shomyo*, its earliest form. The other base was the seventh-century "foreign" music of courtly China. Of course, Japan had the advantage of working from living foreign traditions, while the West was dealing with the dead-past glories of Greece. Nevertheless, I think it is fascinating to note the rather similar origins of the two traditions as well as the rather similar ages of Western and Japanese art music. While the solid music histories of both traditions are some twelve hundred years old, the uniqueness of the Japanese case is, as mentioned before, that it has been able to preserve living examples from all along the way, with *shomyo* and Gagaku standing at the very beginning and pointing the way toward the future developments of Japanese music as well as hinting at the lost mainland traditions that must have lain behind them. Despite the most diligent work of Western musicologists, we have only recently come close to such a knowledgeable position in the understanding of Western music.

Looking at some of the musical instruments of Gagaku, one can find connections with many parts of Asia. The *biwa* (lute) had definite Near Eastern ancestors, while the *kugo* harp preserved in the Shoso-in can be traced to the bas-reliefs of ancient Assyria. From our earlier discussion of Gagaku history one would expect, of course, many instrumental survivals of T'ang-dynasty China in Japan. Our direct knowledge of such instruments is derived from T'ang writings and from a few Sung-dynasty paintings said to depict T'ang court scenes. Some of the instruments, such as the *biwa*, still exist in both mainland and

Japanese forms. Others, such as the hourglass-shaped drum, are rare now in the land of their origin. Thus when one views the *san no tsuzumi* drum in the Komagaku ensemble, one sees not only the sole survivor among four similarly shaped drums used in the Nara period but also, along with the Korean *changko* drum, a relative of instruments pictured in Buddhist frescoes all over China and far westward along the trade routes to China as well.

The *hichiriki* double reed used in Gagaku today is also a survivor of two earlier models. For me it is of particular interest because its nearest direct relative seems to be the *balavan* folk instrument played in Iran, though its reed is somewhat similar in construction to others found in China and Korea. The shape of the *hichiriki* is unique, the instrument being widest at the reed end. This characteristic is not found in the *piri* of Korea or in the Chinese *kuan tzu*, which are quite straight. The Islamic-related instruments of the Chinese oboe (*sona*) type are different again from either of these shapes, for they have flaring bells and reeds more like those of the Western oboe. Thus the *hichiriki* alone, with the possible exception of a Near Eastern folkloric instrument, seems to preserve a manner of instrument construction known in earlier times on the mainland of Asia but now quite forgotten. The flutes of Gagaku likewise have certain features of construction—for example, their bark wrappings and oval, concave finger holes—which are no longer common in Asian flutes.

The *sho* mouth organ, in contrast with the *hichiriki*, has many relatives in Asia. They range from tribal instruments in Borneo and the jungles of Southeast Asia to the popular *khaen* of Southeast Asia, the *saenghwang* of Korean court music, and the *sheng*, popular in China for everything from a folk song to a modern concerto. What gives the Japanese *sho* its distinct flavor is its use of harmony. The *khaen* of Southeast Asia plays rather solid dronelike chords beneath a melody, while the *sheng* of China today concentrates on parallel-fifth harmonies with occasional interjections of larger chords. The Japanese *sho*, however, as presently used, plays sequences of chords chosen by matching the note at the bottom of the chord with the melody note. The eleven chords available on the *sho* today do not make chord progressions in the Western sense but instead form a succession of harmonic sounds rather like those of the music of Machaut in fourteenth-century Europe. These chords are more of a changing textural matrix in which melodies are set than they are a harmonization of a melody. Certainly they are one of the unique sound characteristics of Gagaku.

The sound of the *dadaiko* drum should also be noted for its unique properties. Two of these giant drums stand in the back corners of the Gagaku room in the Imperial Palace compound. They are used only for certain dance pieces and play the beats normally assigned to the regular Gagaku drum, the *taiko*. Because of the immense size of the drumheads, the sound produced by the *dadaiko* is a rather dull, vibrating thud. By itself, this sound might not be impressive, but in the context of a Bugaku dance composition it is most useful. The effect is quite striking when a dancer shifts his weight from his heel to his toes to the accompaniment of these deep sounds. The drum beats add a grandeur to the movement which is as much psychological as it is musical.

The use of the *dadaiko* drum illustrates a principle common to many forms of Japanese music and to other Japanese art forms as well. This is a general desire to create the maximum effect with a minimum amount of material. When we speak of the changes in the Gagaku tradition, for example, we note that some of them have been motivated by this attitude, so that losses have been turned into new kinds of aesthetic gains. The performance practice on the *biwa* is a good case in point. This lute is capable of many lively and complicated sounds, and there are indications that fanciful improvisations may originally have been common in the playing of the *biwa* within the Gagaku ensemble. The part books for the *biwa,* however, give only the barest outline of what is to be played, and today the performers play only what is notated. This produces a simple strummed arpeggio plus one or two afternotes. One could certainly call this a decay of the tradition, but the musicians have turned it into an aesthetic experience by playing their few notes with great seriousness and style. The manner in which the arm rises and the plectrum crosses the strings is carefully devised so as to indicate that the sound produced is important and also that the gesture used is beautiful. This kind of "choreography" of an instrumental performance suggests yet another characteristic worth noting. In Gagaku, as in other forms of Japanese music, the manner in which one performs is as important as the notes one produces. This attitude enables the seated, basically static musicians of Gagaku to produce a pleasing visual image as well as an aural impression. It is the music itself, however, which is obviously the core of the tradition, so we turn now to the special sound characteristics of Gagaku.

Gagaku illustrates what can be called the chamber-music sound ideal. This means that the basic musical texture of Japanese ensembles is so arranged that every part is meant to be heard. From the standpoint of instrumentation the Gagaku ensemble is certainly an orchestra, since it has several instruments present in each of the basic families: the percussion, the winds, and the strings. But when they play together their tone colors do not blend. The sound of each instrument remains distinct. Once more one is reminded of the music of fourteenth-century Europe, in which strings, flutes, trombones, and bagpipes could be heard playing together. The sounds in both the European music and the Japanese music run parallel, like threads in a multicolored cloth. By not blending as they do in the nineteenth-century Western orchestra, they help us to hear each detail of the music.

In Gagaku the flute and the *hichiriki* performances of a given melody are not the same. Because of their difference in tone color it is possible to hear the two versions of the same melody at the same time. The nuances of these two lines are very subtle, and, once one is aware of them, they can reveal to the listener a great variety of melodic style.

One of the most striking sound characteristics of Gagaku is the way melodic lines seem to float in and out of the chord sounds of the *sho*. The constant crescendos and decrescendos of the *sho* and its smooth changes of chord under held melodic notes give a special sustaining power to what might otherwise be a rather thin sound. In this light it is interesting to compare the full Togaku sound with that of pieces like *Konju no Ha* in which the chordal underpinning of the *sho* is not used.

The *koto* (thirteen-stringed zither with movable bridges) and the *biwa* do not play a melodic part in the modern performance of Gagaku. Rather, they mark off time units in the music by entering on certain stereotyped patterns chosen in relation to the note of the melody appearing at that moment. The *shoko* (gong) and the *taiko* also mark off time units. While the ancient performance practice may have been different, one cannot help being struck by the manner in which today's Gagaku music moves, so to speak, from pillar to pillar of instrumental time-marking sound. The expectation created by an awareness of this progression does much to give the music that sense of forward movement so necessary in all music.

Given the ancient origins of Gagaku, it is interesting to compare this emphasis on the temporal divisions of music by the entrance of specific sounds in a specific order with similar principles found in the orchestras of Southeast Asia and the *gamelans* of Indonesia. In these ensembles certain gongs and drums serve the same functions. Musical time signals of this sort are not common in Western, Near Eastern, or Indian music. They are very common in Southeast Asia, but in Japan they are characteristic only of Gagaku. Could this principle be evidence of a link between ancient traditions hitherto thought of as relatively independent? Is it a principle transferred via China between two distant worlds? Or is it merely an accidental similarity brought on by a decay in the Gagaku tradition? We do not yet know the answers to such questions, but once more one is impressed by the many cultural and historical implications of Gagaku.

From our discussion of the marking of time units, a reader unfamiliar with the Gagaku sound might think that Gagaku is very steady and metronomic. The rhythmic style of the accompaniment of Bugaku (court dance) is, indeed, quite steady and sometimes relatively lively. However, the concert style of Gagaku, when played at its best, is characterized by what can be called breath rhythm. Of course very free tempos can be found in some instances like that of the *netori*, an opening selection played to set the qualities of a mode for the piece that follows if that mode differs from the one of the previous piece or if a performance is beginning. Breath rhythm operates in a *netori* to some extent also, but it is most evident in the opening few minutes of a composition proper. The beginning of *Etenraku* in the Togaku repertoire is typical. In this piece the flute begins with only the percussion for accompaniment in a framework of four widely spaced beats. At the first percussion entrance after the flute opening, the *kakko* (small horizontal drum) begins a very slow drum roll which ends on the next beat, when the main beat of the *taiko* is heard. The appearance of this beat, however, is delayed by all the performers in a manner which can only be described as being like the taking of a deep breath, holding it, and exhaling. Such a beat would be impossible to conduct, yet the performers play the beat together with great skill. They can give each other no visual signals, for, as the pictures in this book show, the performers are seated in rows and cannot see one another. The only way they can really execute such a beat together is to breathe together. Of course, this kind of ensemble nuance is also a part of the chamber-music sound ideal mentioned earlier, for it implies a careful awareness on the part of the players of one another's performance.

The aural and respiratory awareness of the ensemble becomes more evident as a piece like *Etenraku* progresses. Two beats after the *taiko* entrance described above, the *sho* and then the *hichiriki* join the sound. The *biwa* and the *koto* follow in turn. This full ensemble still executes the same exquisite breath control as before the sound of the *taiko*, until the piece is gradually brought to a full and steady tempo. At the final *taiko* beat the sound once more is delayed by such a breath pause. At this point the music gradually begins to fade away until only a pluck of the *biwa* and the *koto* remain to close the piece. Even between these last simple sounds one can feel an aesthetic pause. The concept of *ma* (interval, rest) found in later forms of Japanese music is evident in principle if not in fact in the final cadences of Gagaku. Taken all together, the general impression that Gagaku produces through this special use of rhythm suggests a heavily robed court nobleman stepping cautiously along a path thickly covered with pine needles.

In truth, one cannot really verbalize very successfully about the music of Gagaku. I have tried to show the special historical and social contexts in which Gagaku developed and in which it now resides. I have also spoken of the unusual aspects of some of the instruments of the ensemble and noted a few points about performance. For all that, Gagaku will remain for most people a musical museum containing a very beautiful collection of old masterpieces. Actually, there are those who would say that the same is true of the Western classical tradition. There is no "creativity" left in the eighteenth-century symphonic form except in the area of the performance of such works. Nevertheless, Westerners, and many Japanese as well, listen to Mozart, Beethoven, and Haydn with great pleasure, enjoying the sounds created by artists long dead. Why not enjoy Gagaku in the same way? Neither Mozart nor Gagaku is directly related to modern life, but both are capable of providing the sensitive modern man with moments of aesthetic pleasure and also of reminding him of the beauties that were left behind in man's mad race for progress. Such pleasures and lessons are the reasons why the traditions of Japan and, for that matter, of all countries should be preserved.

Gagaku is no better known to the general Japanese populace than the Pro-Musica medieval-music ensemble of New York is known in America. But let us never judge the importance of either ensemble on the basis of its mass appeal. The world is richer because Japan has done as well as she has in preserving the cultural heritage of her past while surging forward into the murky waters of the modern world. The quiet pools of Gagaku music are refreshing indeed.

GAGAKU

CHAPTER 1

What Is Gagaku?

The Morning of a Public Performance

THE WEATHER WAS LOVELY—as much of it, that is, as I could see from my cramped position aboard one of those supercrowded commuter trains headed for Tokyo Station. The moment we arrived, I was spewed forth along with several hundreds of fellow passengers. By the time I retrieved the package I had been carrying under my arm and regained my balance, the clock directly above my head showed on its freshly scrubbed face that the time was 8:45 A.M. On the way through the surging throng out to the north exit and to the taxi stop, I met four or five of my fellow performers. We all agreed that something must be done to relieve the crowded condition of rush-hour trains and decided that we would all share a single taxi to the Gagaku theater inside the Imperial Palace grounds, where we were to perform together that day. Each of us had a similar package under his arm. They contained the pure-white undergarments, sashes, and *tabi* socks that make up the base for our stage costumes.

Our cab soon arrived at the cream-colored building inside the Hommaru section of the Imperial Palace grounds. This building has been the headquarters of the Department of Music of the Imperial Household Agency for many years, and it contains the theater where public performances of Gagaku have

31

been presented every spring and fall, for three days each, since about 1953. The schedule of performances is always announced in the newspapers and on radio and TV a month or so in advance. Tickets are free of charge, but in order to obtain one it is necessary to send a request by postcard. The office of the Department of Music had been busy for several days answering requests and making last-minute preparations.

When our taxi let us off at the entrance, we noticed that the graveled space in front of the theater, as well as the lobby itself, was already filled with eager Gagaku-lovers. Our theater covers approximately seventy-two square yards and is about eighty-two feet high. The stage is a large square area in the center of the main room of the building. It is elevated a little over three feet above the main level of the theater (although it gives the illusion of being higher), has gravel spread on the floor around it (similar to that found around the Noh stage), and has two huge and highly decorated drums at its upstage corners.

We who work and rehearse in this environment every day have become so used to the peculiar appearance of the stage that we don't even notice it, but those who view it for the first time are fascinated with its mystic atmosphere and have many questions to ask about its decorations and accoutrements. The skylight directly above the stage, which lets in natural light from outside, and the gravel on the floor around the stage remind us that Gagaku was originally presented in the open air—in the gardens of the nobility or within the precincts of important shrines.

A closer look at the stage itself makes one realize that what seemed at first glance to be at eye level is actually only a little more than three feet high. Its red railing, which runs all the way around, except for the entrances at upstage and downstage center, is responsible for giving the impression of greater height. Both front and back entrances have short flights of three steps each, about six feet wide, to provide access to the performing area. The outer edge of the stage measures almost twenty-six feet per side, but the actual performing area is an eighteen-foot-square space in the center which is raised about six inches above the floor of the main stage and is covered with patterned green cloth. The approximately four-foot-wide area around the raised space is covered with white cloth.

The heads of the huge drums at the upstage corners are about six feet in diameter and are decorated with circular designs painted in gold on black: the drum to the left of the audience with a pattern of three comma shapes within a circle, the one to the right of the audience with a similar pattern using two comma shapes. Colorful relief carvings cover the frames: dragons on the left-side drum and phoenixes on the right-side one. At the very top of each drum is a pole, slightly over three feet tall, crowned with a carving: a sun for the drum on the left, a moon for the drum on the right. These drums are known as the great drum of the left and the great drum of the right. On the side of the great drums away from the stage there are smaller drums called *daishoko* which are made in the same style. In front of the right-hand *daishoko* is placed a signboard on which the program for the day is announced.

Behind the stage proper is hung a curtain with a pattern of crests and vertical stripes. When the orchestra provides accompaniment for the dances on a Gagaku program, the musicians, called *kangata,* are seated on special stools directly in front of this curtain. For purely orchestral numbers, of course, they occupy the center of the stage.

As noted above, a rather large number of people had already

arrived on this particular morning, even though it was still more than an hour before performance time. People of all ages from all parts of the country, and even some from foreign countries, were taking their time choosing seats, reading the programs they had received at the entrance, and studying the stage.

The Classifications of Gagaku

As the characters of its name indicate (*ga* means "elegant," and *gaku* means "music"), Gagaku is a dignified, highly refined, elegant style of music and dance. It is performed at an excruciatingly leisurely tempo.

Gagaku is divided into three general classifications. The first group is made up of vocal music and includes *kagura, azuma asobi,* Yamato *mai,* and the like. Simple dances are performed to some of the pieces in this group. The music itself is derived from the oldest forms of true Japanese music and is used in the ancient rituals and festivals celebrated in the Imperial Palace.

The second group comprises instrumental music. Some fourteen hundred years ago, various styles of music and dance were imported from the Asian continent. They were then adapted to satisfy the tastes of the Japanese, and new works were composed in the resulting assimilated style. The pieces imported from China and Vietnam are known today as Togaku, and those from Korea and the kingdom of P'o-hai (in Japanese, Bokkai) are called Komagaku.

The third group consists of ancient Japanese vocal music known as *saibara* and *roei*—music that flourished around the middle of the Heian period (794–1185). Pieces from the second

8. Ryo-o: *a dance of the left*

9. *Bugaku performance by imperial Gagaku troupe, Tokyo*

12. *Gagaku orchestra accompanying a Bugaku dance*

17. *Playing the* dadaiko

18. *Dance properties: lance and shield for Bairo*

19 (top left). *Playing the* shoko

20 (top right). *Playing the* tsuri-daiko

21 (bottom left). *Playing the* kakko

22 (opposite page). *Musicians in costume* ▷
for orchestral performance

24 (top). Playing the biwa
25 (bottom). Finger picks for the so

◁ *23 (opposite page). Playing the* so

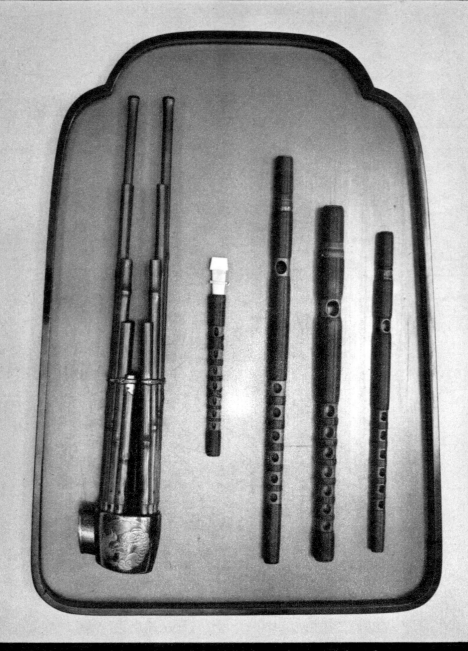

26. *Wind instruments (left to right):* sho, hichiriki, kagurabue, oteki, komabue

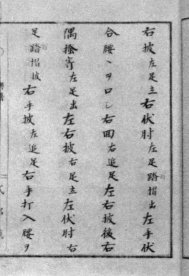

27. Dance score for Manzairaku

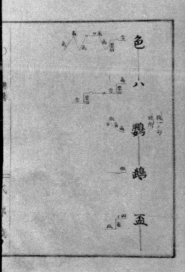
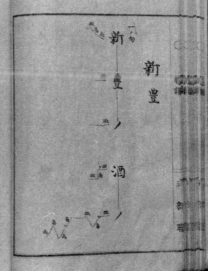

28. Vocal score for roe

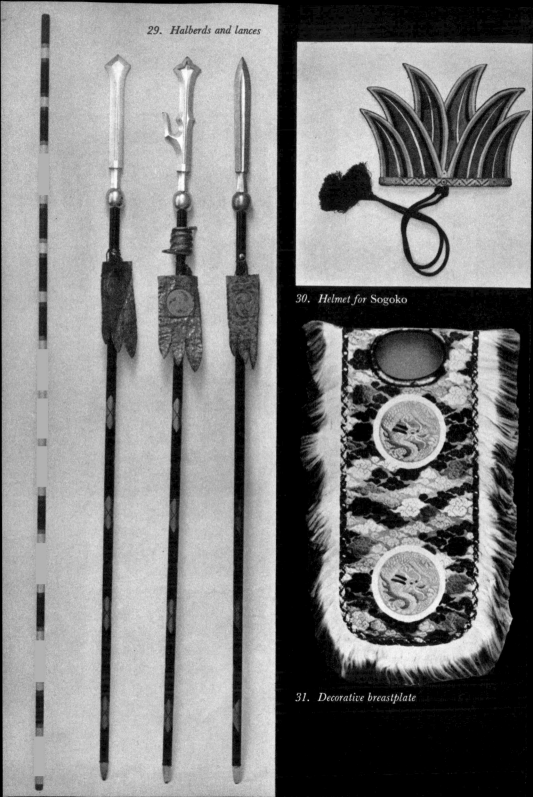

29. Halberds and lances

30. Helmet for Sogoko

31. Decorative breastplate

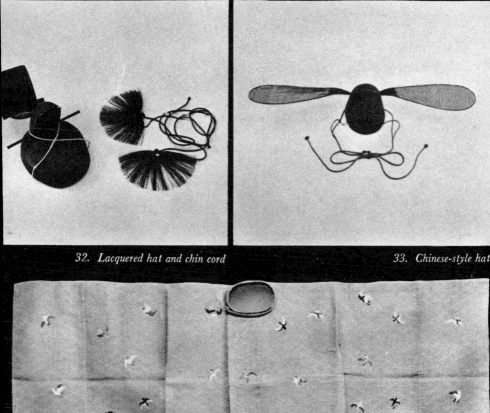

32. *Lacquered hat and chin cord*   33. *Chinese-style hat*

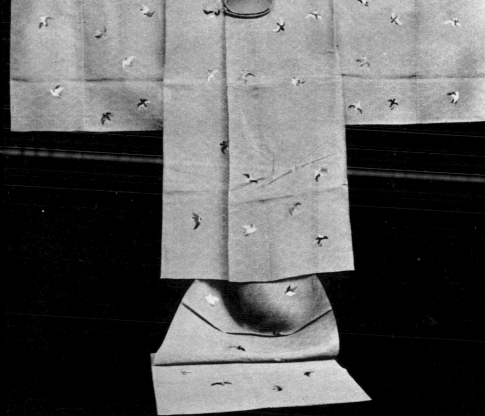

35. Hassen *mask*

36. Nasori *mask*

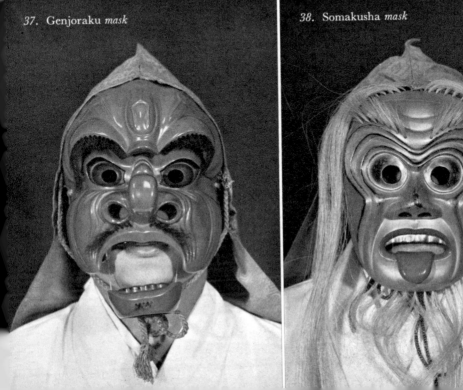

37. Genjoraku *mask*

38. Somakusha *mask*

39. Saisoro *mask*

40. Kitoku *mask*

41. *General-purpose mask*

42. Kotokuraku *mask*

43. Ryo-o *mask*

and third groups are used mainly for banquets inside the Imperial Palace. The some three hundred works in the present Gagaku repertoire have been passed down, through various stages of prosperity and decay, under the patronage of the imperial family and the aristocracy.

As I walked into the lobby of the theater, I found a group of college students deep in a lively discussion. Let me try to reproduce what I heard.

STUDENT A: They say the mainstream of present-day Japanese Gagaku is Togaku. This Togaku originally came from ancient China, didn't it?

STUDENT B: That's what they say. About twenty-five hundred years ago, Confucius taught that decorum brings about discipline in the universe and that music contributes harmony. He himself is said to have been very fond of the lute. Maybe Gagaku was originally based on Confucian principles.

STUDENT C: But I've heard that the music used for funerals and other ceremonies in Confucius' lifetime was not imported into Japan.

STUDENT A: That's right. It was banquet music that was introduced into Japan—music that flourished in western China during the T'ang dynasty. It seems that the music that came to Japan was the most brilliant and showy—that is, compared to other styles of music of those times.

STUDENT C: Then, compared to Gagaku, the history of Western music is very short, isn't it?

STUDENT D: Bach is called the father of modern Western music, and he lived during the eighteenth century. That's about the middle of the Edo period in Japanese history.

STUDENT B: And then there were the classicists like Mozart and after them the romanticists. They all composed music based on the major and minor scales. And then, around the beginning of the twentieth century, composers began to write atonal and twelve-tone-scale music.

STUDENT C: I read somewhere that Debussy's impressionistic music was influenced by Gagaku.

STUDENT D: It seems that Western music has always been based on strict rules of logic, but certainly Eastern music and logic have never been compatible.

STUDENT E: You can't expect Gagaku to show development and modernization, since it was kept away from the public for so many centuries. Why, it's only in the last few years that anyone outside the imperial family knew much more about Gagaku than its name. In fact, serious research on Gagaku is just beginning to be carried out.

Student knowledge-and-fact-comparing discussions like this one can go on forever. They seemed to be having such a good time together that I went quietly on after a moment or two of listening and climbed the stairs to the second-floor lobby, where still other spectators had gathered.

String and Percussion Instruments

On the second floor of the theater, in the hall directly behind the seats facing the front of the stage, is a display of Gagaku instruments, masks, and costumes. An old man was peering into the display case that holds the instruments and talking to himself.

"I wonder if they still use these instruments."

Without thinking, I answered, "Yes, we do."

The old man looked around and said, "Oh, you must be one of the musicians. Am I glad to see you! Hey, you two! Come on over here. This musician is going to tell us about the instruments."

A boy who looked like a junior high school student and a young lady who looked like his older sister came hurrying over. A few other people in the lobby had also heard the old man, and the whole group surrounded me with eager faces full of interest. The old man ignored my panic-stricken, trapped expression and launched into what seemed like the beginning of a long list of questions.

OLD MAN: This *biwa* seems somewhat larger than average instruments of the type.

TOGI (MYSELF): Yes, it is. It's called a *gaku biwa*.

SPECTATOR A: I suppose it must be the ancestor of the Heike *biwa* and the Satsuma *biwa*.

TOGI: Well, yes, that's true. The *gaku biwa* is somewhat different from others of the *biwa* family in that it is held in a vertical position and strummed with a large plectrum. It has four bridges and four strings and has a range of twenty notes in the lower register.

SPECTATOR B: What is the plectrum made of?

TOGI: Ivory. The shell of the *biwa* is usually made of mulberry wood, but some are of rosewood.

At this point I resigned myself to the fact that I would have to give a complete lecture before my audience was satisfied; so I began to rack my brain for all the information I could remember.

TOGI: The *biwa* originated in Central Asia. It was later introduced into China, where it was called the *pipa*, and then into Japan. The Japanese either misheard or could not pronounce the Chinese name. Thus the instrument came to be called the *biwa* in Japan. There are several excellent examples of early *biwa* in the Shoso-in treasure house in Nara.

SPECTATOR A: That little drum on the stand is a *kakko*, isn't it?

SPECTATOR B: It has two heads, and its body is shaped like an hourglass. Is it tuned by means of the strings that go between the heads?

TOGI: No. The strings are only tightened enough to make the pitch of both heads the same. It is played by striking both heads lightly with the drumsticks.

The junior high school student finally mustered up enough courage to ask a question.

JUNIOR HIGH SCHOOL STUDENT: My music teacher at school said that the *kakko* player is the conductor of the orchestra. Is that true?

TOGI: Yes, that's right. The *kakko* sets the tempo for the whole performance. The man who plays it must be very well trained and highly experienced.

YOUNG LADY: Did the *kakko* also come from China?

TOGI: There is a legend that one of the emperors during the T'ang dynasty was a very good *kakko* player. The *kakko* is used in Togaku, and the *san no tsuzumi,* the drum you see next to it, is used in Komagaku.

SPECTATOR B: Are there other instruments that are used only in Togaku or only in Komagaku?

TOGI: Generally speaking, in Togaku the reed instruments used are the *sho,* the *hichiriki,* and the *oteki;* the string instruments used are the *biwa* and the *koto*; and the percussion instruments used are the *kakko*, the *taiko*, and the *shoko*. In Komagaku only two reed instruments—the *komabue* and the *hichiriki*—and three percussion instruments—the *san no tsuzumi*, the *taiko*, and the *shoko*—are used.

SPECTATOR B: Is the *san no tsuzumi* played with only one stick?

TOGI: Yes, that's right.

OLD MAN: Isn't this *taiko* rather small?

TOGI: Yes. It's for indoor use. As you can see, it is hung from a frame. For this reason it is called a *tsuri-daiko*. Do you see the paintings of Chinese lions on it? The huge drums you can see at the upstage corners of the stage are for outdoor use, and there is another type of drum called the *ninai-daiko* which is for use in parades.

JUNIOR HIGH SCHOOL STUDENT: Are they all played with two sticks?

TOGI: Yes. The left is struck first, rather lightly. Then the right is struck with a strong beat. The *shoko* is also struck with two sticks, but in a sort of scraping motion.

We all moved together to the next showcase.

JUNIOR HIGH SCHOOL STUDENT: Hey! That *koto* looks just like the one my big sister plays.

OLDER SISTER: Yes, it does. But I think the bridges are a little narrower.

TOGI: And the strings, which are made of silk, are a little thicker than those used for the ordinary *koto* today. Also the bamboo picks are quite different. Watch during the performance, and you will see the difference in playing technique.

OLDER SISTER: Is it true that the Gagaku *koto* is called a *gakuso*?

TOGI: Yes, it is. During the Ch'in dynasty in China, over two thousand years ago, both twelve-stringed and thirteen-stringed instruments were used. It was the thirteen-stringed one that was introduced into Japan and is still used in much the same form today. It seems that the Chinese thought of the *koto* as a dragon, because the parts of the instrument are named for the parts of a dragon's body: dragon's head, dragon's tongue, dragon's tail, and the like.

SPECTATOR C: *Koto* are made of paulownia wood, aren't they? . . . Oh! Those *koto* over there have only six strings.

TOGI: They're called *wagon* or Yamato *koto*. The *wagon* is the only Gagaku instrument that actually originated in Japan. It is said that even before the days of the legendary emperor Jimmu the Japanese made music by strumming the strings of six bows that were lined up next to one another.

SPECTATOR A: The bridges are quite unusual, aren't they?

TOGI: They're made from V-shaped maple branches, and the bark is left on the back side. The *wagon* is played by means of a tortoise-shell plectrum that is drawn across the strings toward the player in a sweeping motion. It is usually played with the right hand, but the left hand is also sometimes used.

OLDER SISTER: In what type of music is the *wagon* used?

TOGI: In the ancient Japanese styles such as *kagura, azuma asobi,* and *kume mai.*

SPECTATOR A: Do you perform the kind of *kagura* that we see at the festivals back home in the country?

TOGI: No. That is technically known as *sato kagura.* We perform only the imperial ceremonial type called *mi-kagura.*

JUNIOR HIGH SCHOOL STUDENT: Where is *mi-kagura* performed inside the Imperial Palace grounds?

TOGI: At the shrine called the Kashiko-dokoro, where the

same god is worshiped as at the Grand Shrine of Ise. This is where the souls of all the former emperors are worshiped. *Mi-kagura* and *azuma asobi* are performed for special ceremonies in the garden in front of the shrine building.

SPECTATOR B: Won't you please tell us a little more about what *mi-kagura* is like? Also about *azuma asobi* and *kume mai*.

TOGI: Yes, I will. But first let me explain one more instrument. Do you see the long, flat pieces of wood standing by the *wagon?* They look something like the flat pieces of wood that Shinto priests carry—the kind that have been split down the center. They are called *shakubyoshi* and are made of hard wood like plum, cherry, or loquat. The solo singers in *kagura uta* and *saibara* use them to beat time.

Songs and Dances of Japanese Origin

The worship of ancestors was a most important aspect of Japanese life in ancient times. Dances and songs in honor of these god-ancestors were always one of the main forms of worship. From around the Nara period (710–84) special all-night performances were given at the imperial court on festive occasions, and, from the middle ages on, performances were also given in supplication for the recovery of emperors from their illnesses and for divine guidance in times of national crisis. At present, *mi-kagura* is performed every year in the middle of December at ceremonies honoring the gods of heaven and earth and the imperial ancestors and on the evenings of the festivals commemorating the emperors Jimmu (Japan's first emperor) and Taisho (father of the present emperor). There are about fifteen pieces in the *mi-kagura* repertoire, including *Niwabi,*

Zoka, Hoshi, Asakura, and *Sonokoma.* Performances begin at sunset and last until the first cock crows on the following morning.

A special temporary stage is set up facing the shrine within the Imperial Palace grounds. Curtains are hung around three sides, leaving only the front open, and the whole scene is lit by bonfires. A total of twenty-four performers line up on both sides of the stage facing each other. Some are instrumentalists, and some are chanters. All are dressed in ancient costumes. One man in the group is designated as the *ninjo,* or conductor. He wears a special costume with a sword in his belt and carries a stalk of pampas grass from which is hung a white circle made of rattan. This circle represents the sacred mirror of Shinto.

Until the Meiji era (1868–1912) the emperor himself always participated in the performances. Some emperors played the *koto* and others the *fue* (flute). Even today the emperor does not sleep while a performance of *mi-kagura* is being presented.

Azuma asobi (eastern dance) is said to have come from the eastern part of the country. It is constructed of five sections: *ichi uta, ni uta, suruga uta, motomeko uta,* and *obire uta.* The *shaku-byoshi,* the *wagon,* the *komabue,* and the *hichiriki* make up the accompanying orchestra for the singers and dancers. During the last half of the *suruga uta* either four or six dancers appear and dance during the remaining sections of the music. They wear long, flowing, solid-colored robes and black lacquered hats and have swords thrust through their belts.

Azuma asobi is performed at the spring and autumn equinoxes in honor of the spirits of former emperors and on the third of April in honor of the first emperor, Jimmu. These performances take place in front of the imperial ancestral shrine in the Imperial Palace compound. The Gagaku troupe also performs *azuma asobi* at the festival of the Hikawa Grand Shrine (Omiya,

Saitama Prefecture) on the first of August, but other grand shrines such as Kamo, Iwashimizu, and Kasuga have their own troupes of musicians and dancers for festival performances.

Kume mai is a song and dance based on Emperor Jimmu's song of victory when he conquered the tribal chieftain Eukashi at Uda. It has three movements: *mairi onjo, agebyoshi,* and *makade onjo.* The singing is accompanied by the *shakubyoshi,* the *wagon,* the *oteki,* and the *hichiriki.* Four performers dressed in red hats and robes dance a highly stylized pantomime of the legendary battle.

Yamato *mai* is an ancient dance from the Yamato district (present Nara Prefecture) of Japan. It is performed every year at the Imperial Palace on the evening before the Harvest Festival in November. The accompanying song says, "I will take the sacred branch and rule for all eternity." The four dancers wear black lacquered hats and solid deep-blue or crimson robes. A small orchestra made up of the *shakubyoshi,* the *oteki,* and the *hichiriki* accompanies the singers and dancers.

Gosechi-no-mai is the only female dance in the repertoire. It is performed on the first day of the grand banquet in celebration of the coronation of a new emperor and is based on a legend that tells of a goddess who appeared before Emperor Temmu as he played the *koto* one evening in the Yoshino Palace. She danced for him, "waving her sleeves five times," according to the legend, and *gosechi-no-mai* is an ancient re-creation of this mythical entertainment. The music is in two parts, and the singers are accompanied by an orchestra made up of the *shakubyoshi,* the *wagon,* the *oteki,* and the *hichiriki.* In ancient days the young women who performed this dance were chosen from the aristocracy by means of a contest known as the *gosechi sadame.*

Wind Instruments

After the preceding interlude of explanation, I once again took up the dialogue with my listeners.

TOGI: Now let's take a look at the middle shelf of that display case. We see three flutes lined up in a row. The longest of the three is used along with the *shakubyoshi* and the *wagon* in *kagura* performances and is called the *kagurabue*. It is thicker than the others and has only six finger holes. The one beside it with seven finger holes has several names: *oteki, ryuteki,* and *omobue*. It is used in the orchestra for Togaku, *kume mai,* and Yamato *mai*. The third flute is the shortest and most slender of all. It is the *komabue* and is used in Komagaku. Like the *kagurabue* it has only six holes. Its range is very high. Nowadays it is sometimes used also in the orchestra for *azuma asobi* in place of the flute called a *chukan*.

OLD MAN: All the flutes seem to be made of bamboo wrapped in white birchbark and lacquered.

TOGI: That's right. Usually the outer skin of the bamboo is taken off, but it is sometimes left on in the case of the *kagurabue*.

SPECTATOR A: The *oteki* looks very much like the flute used in Noh.

TOGI: Well, the basic structure is the same, but in the Noh flute the section between the mouthpiece and the finger holes is narrower than the rest of the instrument, and this makes the tone quality quite different. Now, next to the flutes is the *hichiriki*. This instrument originated in West Asia and then, by way of Central Asia, finally reached China. At the time when it was introduced into Japan from China there were two sizes of *hichiriki*. The larger size, called the *ohichiriki*, was popular during the early Heian period and is mentioned in *The Tale of Genji*. Today, however, only the smaller size is used. The construction of the body is quite similar to that of the flutes. The greatest difference is that it is thicker at the mouthpiece end. It has seven finger holes on top and two on the other side.

SPECTATOR B: It looks awfully short. Exactly how long is it?

TOGI: Just a little over seven inches. It has a double reed made of rushes and inserted in the head end. The best rushes are said to come from the Yodo River in Osaka.

JUNIOR HIGH SCHOOL STUDENT: The double reed looks something like the one in an oboe. Is the sound similar too?

TOGI: It has a loud, sharp sound and a narrow range in the medium register. But it can produce smooth, flowing sounds too.

Just as I was ready to begin talking about the *sho,* a foreign lady came up, took one look at it, then smiled at me and said, "Oh, it's a mouth organ." The *sho* is probably the best known among all the Gagaku instruments.

SPECTATOR C: Is this the instrument that's mentioned in the famous lullaby?

TOGI: Yes, it is. The type we use today is made up of seventeen bamboo pipes placed in a circle. Underneath is a bowl-shaped section with a mouthpiece.

JUNIOR HIGH SCHOOL STUDENT: How do you play it?

TOGI: There are metal vibrators on the bottom ends of fifteen of the pipes. The metal is painted with a chemical that is very sensitive to moisture; so the *sho* must be heated over a charcoal fire just before it is played. Otherwise it will produce no sound. There are small finger holes in all the pipes. When the holes are closed, the pipes will produce sound when air is blown or sucked through the mouthpiece. When the holes are all open, no sound at all can be made. Usually five or six pipes are sounded together in a prolonged chord. Melodies can also be played by sounding one pipe at a time. The one-pipe technique is used in the accompaniment for such vocal music as *saibara* and *roei*.

OLD MAN: Oh, I just remembered. When I was a boy, I had a picture book with a picture of a Minamoto general standing on a mountain and playing this instrument.

TOGI: It must have been an illustration of the legend of Shiragi Saburo. He owned the famous *sho* called Majie-maru.

Music Notation

JUNIOR HIGH SCHOOL STUDENT: Does the Gagaku orchestra use sheet music during a performance the way a Western-style orchestra does?

TOGI: Sheet music? Well, no. Music notation was originally used only as a memory aid in Gagaku, and even today it is very simple. In fact, it is useless unless the performer has a solid background of training in the use of the instrument and has memorized the piece beforehand. A student is first trained to sing the parts for the instrument he is to learn. Only after he has learned to produce the piece is he taught the techniques of playing the instrument. In other words, the professional performer is required to memorize the whole repertoire.

Kangen and Bugaku

During the above conversation young boys wearing white kimono and light-blue *hakama* (full, skirtlike trousers) were busily bringing instruments onto the stage and lining them up in proper order for the orchestra. In the front row were the *kakko,* the *taiko,* and the *sho,* followed by the *biwa* and the *koto* in the second row, and, in the third row, white porcelain charcoal braziers for warming the *sho.* The boys brought in two of each kind of instrument.

The program for the day read as follows:

> Part 1. *Kangen* (orchestral music):
> *Hyojo no Netori*
> *Saibara: Ise no Umi*
> *Gojoraku no Kyu*
> *Bairo*
> Part 2. *Bugaku* (dances):
> *Embu*
> *Manzairaku*
> *Nasori*

Finally the musicians came onstage and took their places behind their instruments.

The first number on the program, *Hyojo no Netori,* means simply "tuning up in the key (or mode) of *hyojo.*" There are six "keys," as we shall call them, in Gagaku: *ichikotsucho, hyojo, sojo, oshikicho, banshikicho,* and *taishikicho.* Each program begins with the *netori* of the key chosen for the day's performance, and all pieces are then played in that key. Generally speaking, the key is chosen in accordance with the season—for example, *sojo* for spring, *oshikicho* for summer, *hyojo* for autumn, and *banshikicho* for winter. The *netori* was originally no more than a practical procedure for tuning the instruments before a performance, just as in a Western orchestra, but it became stylized and is now a short, rhythmless piece of music. When a larger orchestra than usual performs, a similar piece called a *choshi* is played.

The *sho* begins the *netori*, followed by a harmonious note from the *hichiriki*, and after they have played together for a short time, the *oteki* joins in along with the *kakko*. Next the *biwa* and the *koto* join in and play together, and the piece is finished with the sounding of the dominant note of the key on the *koto*.

A *kangen* program—that is, a program of orchestral music—is generally planned with solemn pieces at the beginning. These are followed by progressively lighter pieces. However, when a *saibara* piece is included, it is always performed immediately after the *netori* or the *choshi*.

Legend has it that *saibara* originated in the songs of packhorse drivers bringing tribute to the capital at Nara. Whether this is true or not, the *saibara* melodies were undoubtedly folk songs that were introduced at court, refined, and arranged for presentation as *kangen* pieces.

Saibara are divided into two groups called *ryo* and *ritsu*. These classifications correspond roughly to the major and minor keys of Western music. *Ise no Umi*, the *saibara* on our program, is a *ritsu* piece and can be played in either *hyojo* or *taishikicho*. *Ryo* numbers are played in the key of *sojo*. *Saibara* include love songs, satirical songs, children's songs, and songs describing local scenery, but the melodies do not express the emotional content of the lyrics. The singing is more like a chant than a song—very

near to everyday conversational voice production. This is true
of all vocal music in Gagaku, especially Japanese-originated
styles such as *saibara, kagura,* and *roei.* The orchestra that accompanies *saibara* is made up of the *shakubyoshi,* the *sho,* the
hichiriki, the *oteki,* the *biwa,* and the *koto.*

The next number on the program for the day was a Togaku
piece called *Gojoraku no Kyu.* Togaku pieces are divided into
three classifications—large, medium, and small—according to
their scope and difficulty. The four most important pieces in the
present Togaku repertoire are *Shunnoden, Ojo, Sogoko,* and
Manjuraku. They are referred to collectively as the *Shika no
Taikyoku.*

Gojoraku is the only piece in the medium classification in the
present repertoire. It has three movements, called *jo, ha,* and
kyu. The *jo* movement is extremely gentle and relaxed; the *ha*
has a medium, flowing tempo; and the *kyu* is brighter, lighter,
and faster. But "fast" in Gagaku still seems very slow and relaxed to people who are accustomed to the tempo and rhythms
of modern life and music. *Gojoraku* was originally composed as a
variation on the five virtues of Confucianism and is performed
both as an orchestral number and as a dance. The *kyu* movement is often performed as an independent piece, as it was on
this day's program—hence *Gojoraku no Kyu,* or "the *kyu* of
Gojoraku."

The last piece on the *kangen* program for the day was *Bairo.*
Most *kangen* pieces are played in a smooth, slurred style known
as *kangen-buki,* while pieces played as accompaniment to Bugaku
dances are performed in a more rhythmical style called Bugaku-
buki. Since *Bairo* is used both as a *kangen* piece and as Bugaku
accompaniment, it can be performed in both styles.

The only type of *kangen* music not included in the day's

program was *roei*: ancient Chinese and Japanese poetry sung to a melody with a soft accompaniment provided by the *sho*, the *hichiriki*, and the *oteki*. *Roei* is performed along with *kangen* pieces in the *ichikotsucho*, the *hyojo*, and the *banshikicho* keys. Each piece is divided into three sections: *ichi no ku*, *ni no ku*, and *san no ku*. The *ni no ku* is sung in an extremely high range. Each section begins with a solo that is joined by the chorus after the first phrase.

After the *kangen* section of the program for the day came the Bugaku section. *Kangen* was always performed by aristocrats more for their own pleasure than for the purpose of playing before an audience. Bugaku, on the other hand, was developed and presented from the very beginning with an audience in mind and was performed in such places as the grounds of various imperial palaces, the precincts of shrines and temples, and the gardens of noblemen's mansions. For this reason, only professional performers from among the common people were allowed to dance. As a result of this custom, Bugaku techniques came to be handed down in families in a manner similar to that of the other traditional performing arts of Japan. Bugaku dances accompanied by the Chinese-originated Togaku are called dances of the left, and those accompanied by the Korean-originated Komagaku are known as dances of the right.

A formal program of Bugaku always begins with *Embu*, a piece performed by one dancer of the left and one dancer of the right. The dance is said to represent an ancient Chinese warrior-emperor in the act of worshiping the gods of heaven and earth in an open field. It serves the same celebratory function as *Okina* in the Noh drama. The oldest dancers or the heads of the

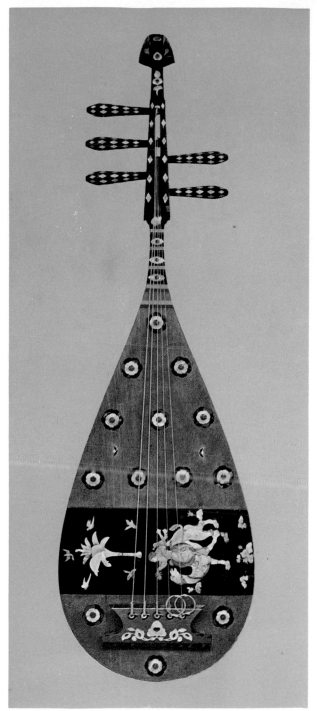

44. *Nara-period* biwa

45. *Painting: Bugaku dancers*

46. *Painting: recital by court women*

47, 48. Painting: Bugaku dances

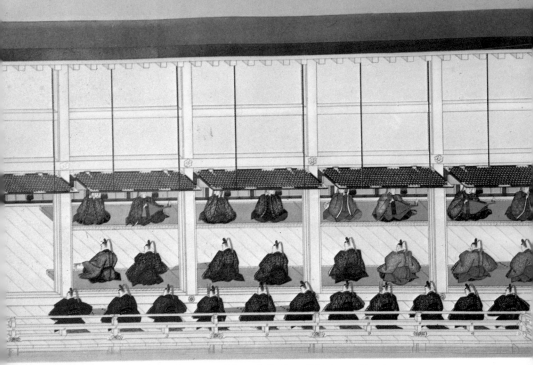

49. *Painting: Gagaku performance with participation of Emperor Komei*

50. *Painting:* mi-kagura *performance with participation of Emperor Komei*

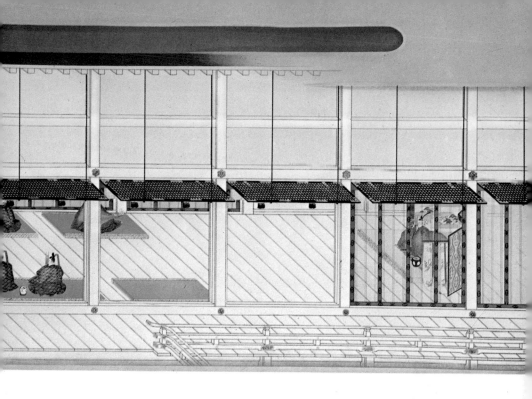

51. *Painting: performance of* kume mai *for Emperor Komei's coronation*

52. *Bonten mask used in ancient* gyodo *procession*

53. *Bronze sculpture: Buddhist angel-musician*

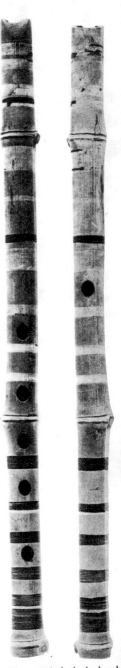

◁ 54. *Nara-period* shakuhachi
(right) and detail

55. *Nara-period* shakuhachi:
side (left) and lower side

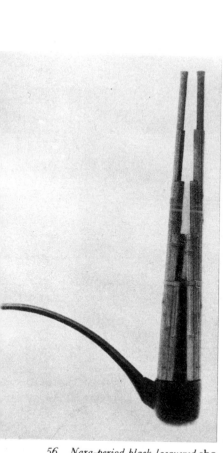

56. *Nara-period black-lacquered* sho

57. *Nara-period* sho *of Chinese bamboo*

58. *Rikishi mask for Gigaku*

59. *Gojo mask for Gigaku*

60. Goko mask for Gigaku

61. *Karura mask for Gigaku*

62. *Bugaku mask for* Sanju

63. *Bugaku mask for* Bato

64. *Bugaku mask for* Onintei

65. *Bugaku mask for* Ama Ni no Mai

66–69. Stone carvings (China): Buddhist angels as musicians

70. Wall painting (China): celestial musicians in Buddhist paradise

夜半樂

乚九　子九　子九　子四九　九四

カ以エ乚い　エ同　乚九　子　九子四九乚四

四　九同同　ツ八ワ乚ス乚ツ乚上九

九子乙エ乚ミ乙ミ　同同同

九子乙子乙七十七ツ七ツ　乚上九四乚

乚ミ乙七乙ヤ乙エ乚一八九乙ミ乙七乙ミ　九乚九四乚五

ヤ一七ヤ九乙一七十七ツ七ツリ乚上九四乚

八九五九子乙子乙四一七　九乚九四乚

七ヤエ一七ヤ

第二　ス七乚四九四乚九

乚エ乚い　ワ乚九四　ス七乚

前取同字彈　第三　九九乚九乚九乚

子九子四九乚四ワエ乚い四乚四乚四

彈　第四　乚九子乙ミ乙え　前取三同字

九四九乚四九乙ミ乙七乙乚九子乚九子九四

九子乚上九五九ワエ乚い　ス四乚四子

乚上九五九　前取二同字彈

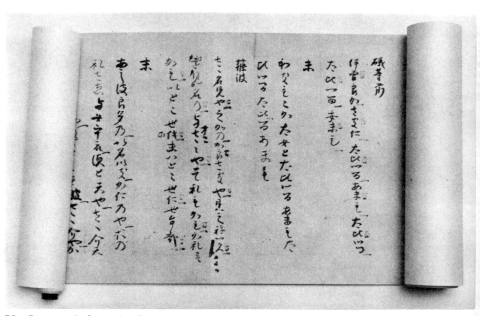

71, 72. *Sections of musical notation for five-stringed* koto

73. *Secret musical notation for* kagura wagon

五絃

調曲并廿七種

平調　一越調

盤沙調

王照君　大食調二種

何滿子　黃鍾調

如意娘　以之調六種

薛問提　夜半樂

崇明樂　六胡州

飲酒樂　天長久

弊界見　惜々塩

九明樂　秦王破陳樂

　　　聖明樂

　　　毘郷堂々

　　　武媚娘

　　　三星

　　　胡詠詞

　　　襪羅蜜

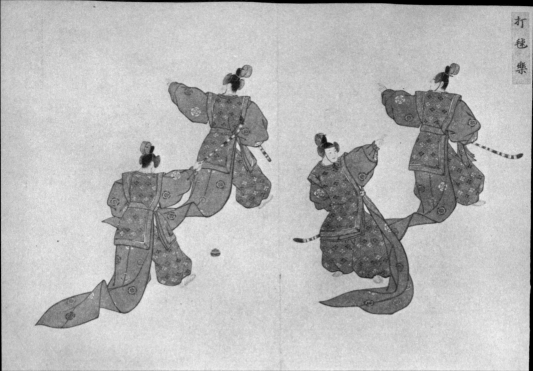

打毬樂

74. *Painting*: Dagyuraku, *a dance of the left*

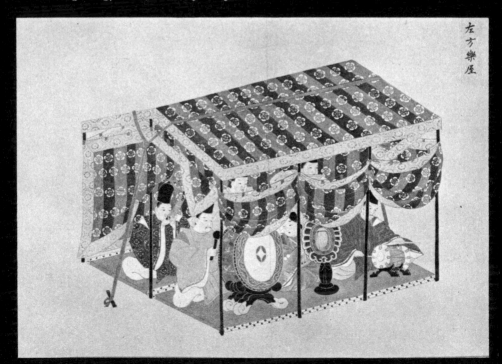

左方樂屋

75. *Painting: tent for musicians of the left*

狛
桙

76. *Painting:* Komaboko, *a dance of the right*

右
方
樂
屋

77. *Painting: tent for musicians of the right*

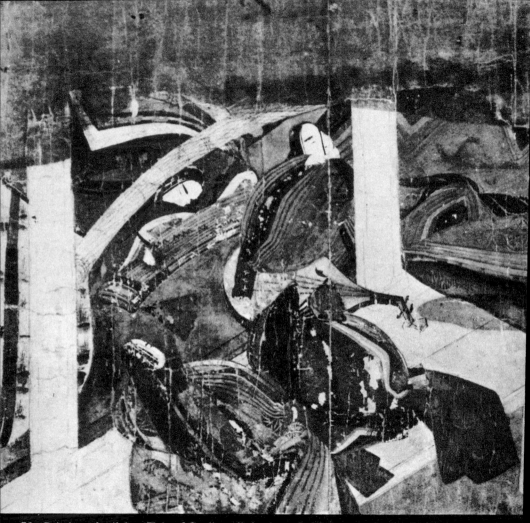

78. *Painting: detail from* Tale of Genji *scroll showing recital by court ladies*

79. *Painting: dancers and musicians performing* Karyobin

80. Painting: *performance of* azuma asobi

81. Painting: performance of Taiheiraku

82. *Reconstruction of antique* kagura *score*   83. *Old record of Gagaku traditions*

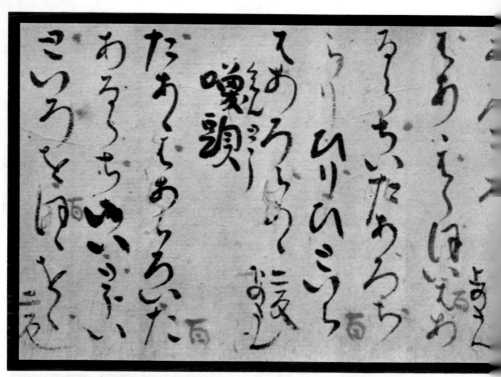

84. *Detail from score of* Etenraku *in handwriting of Emperor Goyozei*

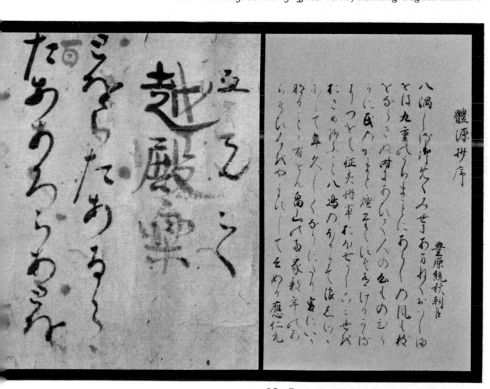

85. *Section from list of official ranks, including Gagaku musicians*

86. *Beginning of Gagaku chronicle* Taigensho

87. *Painting:* Embu, *a congratulatory halberd dance*

88. *Painting: Gagaku performance for shogunate officials*

89. Painting: dance for Festival of the White Horse

90. Painting: Gagaku performance for New Year's

91. *Painting: Bugaku dancers on horseback at Kitano Shrine*

92. *Painting:* mi-kagura *at Kamo Shrine*

93. *Painting: Bugaku at Kamo Shrine*

94. *Painting: Gagaku performance at Kyoto Imperial Palace*

95. *Painting: native dances performed for coronation of new emperor*

96. *Painting: Gagaku performance at Kyoto Imperial Palace*

97. *Woodblock print: Gagaku musicians and dancer*

two troupes—that is, the troupes of dancers of the left and of the right—are the only ones allowed to perform *Embu*.

There are four classifications in Bugaku: *bun no mai* (literary dances), *bu no mai* (warrior dances), *hashiri mai* (running dances), and *dobu* (child dances). The general feeling or texture of the various classifications is sufficiently indicated in the literal meanings of their names. Examples of dances of the left in the four classifications are *Manzairaku, Taiheiraku, Ranryo-o,* and *Karyobin,* respectively; examples of dances of the right are *Engiraku, Bairo, Nasori,* and *Kocho.*

After *Embu,* dances of the left and the right are performed alternately, with an equal number of each on the program. Consequently the next number on our program for the day was *Manzairaku,* a dance of the left. After an orchestral prelude, either four or six dancers enter the stage from behind the upstage-right drum and perform a short solo dance one at a time at the center of the stage. They are dressed in red robes and large helmets. After all have danced their solos, they take their places at the four corners of the stage, face front, and wait for the last strains of the music to end. Then, when the next movement of the music has begun, they dance in unison, leaving the stage one at a time during the closing phrase of the music. This dance tells the story of a phoenix that appeared to an emperor of China during the T'ang dynasty and blessed his reign with lasting peace and long life. The dancers' costumes represent the phoenix itself. *Manzairaku* is a representative *bun no mai* (literary dance) that is performed along with *Taiheiraku,* a *bu no mai* (warrior dance), at the grand banquet held for the coronation of a new emperor.

The last number on the day's program was *Nasori,* a dance of the right. After an orchestral prelude, the main part of the music begins, and two dancers enter the stage from behind the up-stage-left drum. They are dressed in basically red costumes with highly decorated brocade breastplates and full trousers. They wear blue masks with sharp silver fangs and hair coming down over the face, and each carries in his right hand a silver mace-like baton with a ball on one end. The dance represents two fierce dragons frolicking and enjoying each other's company. The duet begins with the dancers facing each other from the opposite sides of the stage and ends with both in a crouching position. *Nasori* can also be performed by a single dancer, in which case it is called *Rakuson*.

My listeners heard me through to the end of this long explanation, and I had the feeling that somehow or other they now understood fairly well what the art called Gagaku was all about. But there was still time for one more question and answer.

Masks and Costumes

The old man was looking up at the numerous Bugaku masks arranged on the topmost shelf of the central display cabinet. "These masks are certainly a lot different from Noh masks, aren't they?" he observed.

I answered by explaining that Bugaku masks, in general, are thought to represent the faces of various continental Asian peoples of ancient times—with certain exaggerations, of course. Among them are bright-red masks, white ones, masks with Roman noses, masks with extremely long noses, masks with the white hair of old age, masks with oddly peaked eyebrows, and the like.

For the most part the masks are made of paulownia wood,

although on rare occasions we may find one made of cypress. They are classified in three groups according to their form: large, middle-sized, and small, although these classifications may sometimes appear arbitrary. Large masks include those for *Rato, Konju, Sanju, Kotoku,* and certain other dances. Among middle-sized masks are those for *Ryo-o,* which is surmounted by either a flying dragon or a supernatural bird; for *Nasori,* which has movable eyebrows and a movable lower jaw; and for *Genjoraku,* which is made up of three separate parts. Examples of small masks are those for *Shinsotoku, Shinsoriko, Onin, Chikyu,* and *Kotokuraku,* the last of which has a movable nose.

In addition to masks representing human beings, there are those that represent animals and birds—for example, the mask for *Hassen,* which portrays a crane with a greatly foreshortened beak and has a tinkling silver bell suspended from it to suggest the bird's cry. Other distinctive masks include those of the joyous mountain god in *Somakusha* and the old man in *Saisoro,* the laughing mask for *Ama Ni no Mai,* the female masks for *Ayagiri,* and the general-purpose paper mask used in *Ama* and certain other dances.

From the mask display we moved on to the next cabinet, which contained a typical costume for a dancer of the left. As I did for my audience of Gagaku spectators, let me list here the items of the costume in the order in which they are put on.

Okuchi: trousers of solid-red glossed silk.

Shikai: shoes of white silk lined with cowhide, soled with straw matting, and tied on with silk cords.

Sashinuki: skirtlike trousers of figured white silk embroidered here and there with a five-color design and tied at the ankles with drawstrings.

Shitagasane: a kimono of patterned white silk with arabesques embodying paulownia and bamboo designs.

Hambi: a garment worn over the *shitagasane* and embroidered with a pattern of diamond shapes enclosing phoenix, paulownia, bamboo, and arabesque motifs.

Fukake: gold-brocade leggings lined with scarlet silk.

Wasure-o: a garment resembling the *okuchi* and put on over the *hambi*.

Uwa no kinu: a sleeveless garment of embroidered red gauze-weave silk.

Kintai: a belt of black-lacquered leather decorated with gold fittings.

Torikabuto: a helmet made of molded paper, covered with gold brocade, lined with red silk, and decorated on the right and left sides with a paulownia crest.

There are also a number of special Bugaku costumes—for example, those derived from the uniforms of the ancient imperial guards; the *ryoto* costume, which features an elaborately embroidered breastplate; costumes representing armor; and costumes for *dobu,* or child dances. Again, there are the costumes for the Bugaku orchestra—different from those worn in purely orchestral performances—and for the singers who accompany certain of the dances. And of course there are such dance properties as halberds, lances, swords, batons, and shields.

One of my listeners commented on the obviously great amount of care that went into the making of Bugaku costumes.

"Yes," I replied. "Fortunately, when Tokyo was heavily bombed during the Pacific War, the Department of Music escaped damage, and everything it owned was safely preserved. If all the costumes, masks, and musical instruments in our storehouse had gone up in smoke, I doubt very much that we would even now be able to give public performances like the one you are attending today—and this in spite of the fact that, in 1955, the Japanese government honored us with the designation of 'living national treasures.' "

At this point, from inside the auditorium, came the announcement that the performance was about to begin. With a brief farewell to my listeners, I rushed off to the dressing room to get into my costume.

CHAPTER 2

A Brief History of Gagaku

Ancient Songs and Dances of Japan

ANCIENT JAPANESE SONGS and dances are spoken of in the myths
and legends found in the eighth-century *Kojiki* and *Nihon Shoki,*
the oldest of existing Japanese chronicles, but nothing is known
about how these songs and dances sounded and looked. A
few hints are found among the *haniwa,* the clay figures placed
around burial mounds in early times. One is sitting with a *koto*
on its lap which it is playing with its right hand; another is
dancing with its left hand raised high and its mouth opened
wide in song; still another is beating a small drum that is tied at
its waist.

The most famous of the early myths tells of the time when the
great goddess Amaterasu became angry and hid herself in a
cave. Since she was the sun goddess, her retirement meant that
the whole world was left in darkness. In order to entice her out
again, the goddess Ame no Uzume performed a song and dance
in front of the cave. This is said to have marked the origin of the
important imperial ceremonial songs and dances called *mi-
kagura* (not to be confused with the *sato kagura* and the *o-kagura*
performed at shrine and village festivals). The musical
instrument called the *wagon* is thought to have appeared during
this same mythological age. It is used in the accompaniment
of all early song and dance styles in Japan.

120

Emperor Jimmu, the legendary first emperor of Japan, who is said to have reigned from 660 to 585 B.C., is credited with composing a song and dance to entertain his soldiers in celebration of the subjugation of the Yamato area (present Nara Prefecture). This composition, although probably mythical, is considered to have been the prototype of the song and dance known as *kume mai*.

Legend has it that some eleven centuries later, during the reigns of the emperors Ankan and Senka (A.D. 531–39), a heavenly maiden descended to dance and sing on a beach in Suruga (present Shizuoka Prefecture). The type of song and dance known as *azuma asobi* (literally, "eastern dance") was created in imitation of that of the heavenly maiden and became the basis for a style developed in the eastern part of the country.

In the Yamato area, which we have just noted as the scene of Emperor Jimmu's victory and the origin of *kume mai,* a style of song and dance known as Yamato *mai* was developed. We are told that one day when Emperor Temmu (reigned 673–86) was playing a Yamato *mai* piece on the *koto* at the Yoshino Detached Palace, he saw a young girl (some say a goddess) on top of a nearby mountain wave her sleeves five times in a most graceful manner. Thus he was inspired to compose the *gosechi-no-mai,* which has been performed since that time at the grand banquet given in honor of the coronation of each new emperor.

Legend also accounts for the origin of another form of court music. The imperial prince Yamato Takeru, who is said to have lived from A.D. 82 to 113, figures in Japanese prehistory as a famous warrior who subdued numerous revolts against his father the emperor. When he died at an early age at Nobono in Ise, we are told, his family composed four poems of lamentation. Later these poems were set to music and became the official dirge for imperial funerals. It is known today as the *Ruika*.

These are the early Japanese songs and dances that later became part of what we know today as Gagaku.

The *wagon*, the *kagura* flute, and the *shakubyoshi*, which are the basic instruments used today for these songs and dances, are all instruments of Japanese origin. But the *hichiriki*, which always carries the melodic line in the accompaniment, was imported from China along with the songs and dances known as Togaku, which make up an important part of Gagaku as we know it today. The use of the *hichiriki* in old Japanese styles of song and dance indicates that such compositions were either revised or restored after the import of foreign music and the subsequent development of Gagaku. Thus the strong influence of Chinese music on early Japanese music during the development of Gagaku becomes quite evident.

Introduction of Foreign Music and Dance

The earliest record of the performance of foreign music in Japan tells of eighty musicians sent from Shiragi (Silla, a kingdom in southeastern Korea) in eighty ships in A.D. 453 to participate in the funeral of Emperor Ingyo. The *Nihon Shoki* states that these musicians followed the cortege from Naniwa (present Osaka) to Asuka (in the present Nara Prefecture), where the emperor's body was laid to rest in the imperial mortuary. This is the first record of an official cultural exchange with the Asian mainland, but, judging from the nearness of Japan to China and the Korean peninsula, it seems logical to assume that there was communication between the Japanese and the peoples of these countries from an even earlier date. At least it is certain that the first ambassador from Mimana, a state in south-central Korea, was sent during the last year of Emperor Sujin's reign, which lasted from 97 to 30 B.C., and that a prince from Shiragi (Silla) named Ame no Hihoko had come to Japan a few years earlier and settled in Tajima (in the present Hyogo Prefecture).

Toward the end of the third century A.D., weavers, other craftsmen, and scholars began to come from Kudara (Paekche, a kingdom in southwestern Korea) to take Japanese citizenship and settle permanently in Japan. It is said that when Emperor Richu (reigned 400–405) fell ill, a doctor was brought from Shiragi to care for him.

The *Nihon Shoki* tells us that four musicians were sent to Japan from Kudara in 554 as replacements for an equal number at the court of Emperor Kimmei. This obviously indicates that musicians from the same kingdom in Korea had been sent to Japan at an earlier date.

Buddhism was introduced into Japan during the reign of the same Emperor Kimmei (reigned 539–71) and within a few decades spread and flourished through the efforts of Prince Shotoku (Shotoku Taishi, 572–622). At first the prince used various types of imported music known as Bangaku in the dedication ceremonies for Buddhist statues. Bangaku is included today in the Komagaku classification of Gagaku.

At the start there were very few who attempted to learn the foreign styles of music and dance and even fewer who became proficient in them. In order to remedy this situation, Prince Shotoku set up a music department at the Shitenno-ji temple in Osaka when it was built in 593. New talent was attracted by the special privileges offered—for example, exemption from taxes and the right to pass one's position on to one's descendants. In connection with the latter privilege, it is interesting to note that there are descendants of members of the original Shitenno-ji music department in the music department of the Imperial Household Agency to this day.

In 612, during the reign of Empress Suiko (reigned 592–628), a musician from Kudara named Mimashi acquired Japanese citizenship. Mimashi had sojourned in China, where he studied Gigaku in the state of Wu on the lower Yangtze River. Having settled in Japan, he was commissioned by the empress to teach Gigaku to a group of young men, chosen by Prince Shotoku, at Sakurai in Yamato Province. Very little is known today about Gigaku except that it was a kind of Buddhist dance-drama processional and that Prince Shotoku considered it a very important part of Buddhist ceremonies and festivals. There are more than one thousand Gigaku masks in existence today at the Shoso-in repository and at the Todai-ji and Horyu-ji temples in Nara, but no music, dance notation, or even any clear explanation of the art is to be found in either China or Japan. A full performance of Gigaku is mentioned in records as late as 752, when all types of performing arts were brought together in a tournamentlike festival for the dedication of the statue known as the Great Buddha at the Todai-ji.

Empress Jito (reigned 690–97) sponsored a performance of a Chinese song-and-dance form called *toka* for the New Year's celebration in 693. *Toka* is still performed today at the Atsuta Shrine in Nagoya. It is a prayer dance in which four dancers pound the earth with their feet for the purpose of quieting the spirits of the dead, exorcising evil, and calling forth good fortune for the coming year.

Chinese music, called Togaku, was introduced into Japan

along with Chinese systems and theories in a wide variety of fields at the time of the Taika Reform in 645. In compliance with the laws promulgated by Emperor Mommu in 701, a music department called the Gagaku-ryo was set up along with other Chinese-style departments of the government. More than four hundred musicians and dancers were given positions in this new department. The importance given to music by the government in those days can be imagined when this number is compared with the twenty-five members to which the Department of Music of the Imperial Household Agency is limited today.

The earliest record of the title of a Togaku piece is found in the chronicle *Shoku Nihongi,* which notes that the composition *Gotei Taiheiraku* was performed at a New Year's banquet for government officials in 702. In 704, Awata no Mahito, who had served as an ambassador to China, brought back the Togaku piece entitled *Odaiha Jinraku.*

In 735, Kibi no Mabi, who had served as ambassador to China for eighteen years, returned to Japan with gifts for Emperor Shomu that included books, weapons, and musical instruments. One of the musical instruments was a copper flute, and among the books was a ten-volume set entitled *A Digest of Musical Matters* (Gakusho Yoroku) as well as musical scores for the various instruments. These books have been carefully preserved in Japan. There are no known copies of them in China at present.

In 736, the priest Bodhisena (in Japanese, Baramon) from Tenjiku (present southern India) and the priest Fattriet (in Japanese, Buttetsu) from Rinyu (present South Vietnam) came to Japan and taught eight famous pieces from the repertoire of Indian and Southeast Asian music and dance to musicians and dancers at the Taian-ji temple in Nara and the Shitenno-ji temple in Osaka. These eight pieces were *Bosatsu, Karyobin, Bato, Bairo, Manjuraku, Ranryo-o, Ama Ni no Mai,* and *Konju,* and all of them, with the exception of *Bosatsu,* are in the present Gagaku repertoire. *Manjuraku* was revived in 1967 and performed at the National Theater in Tokyo. This was the first time it had been performed since the turn of the century.

A few years before the arrival of Bodhisena and Fattriet—in 727, to be exact—an ambassador from the land known to the Japanese as Bokkai (part of present Manchuria) came to visit the court of Emperor Shomu. There is no trace left of Bokkai today except in the Japanese name of a bay on the Yellow Sea, but from around the beginning of the eighth century and well into the tenth it was a strong country whose territory extended from the northwestern part of present-day Korea all the way to the western part of present Manchuria. Its Chinese name was P'o-hai.

Official delegations were sent back and forth between Bokkai and Japan some twenty times. Gifts were sent from Bokkai to Japan on all important official occasions, and trade flourished between the two countries. Because of the fragility of the small ships of those days and the rough seas on the southern trade routes, the land route across Bokkai and the short expanse of the calm waters of the Japan Sea came to be used exclusively for trade and official delegations between Japan and all the countries of the Chinese mainland and the Korean peninsula. As a result, in 746 more than one thousand people from Bokkai emigrated to Japan. It is thought that the music known as Bokkaigaku was introduced into Japan at the same time. Later, during the Heian period (794–1185), Bokkaigaku was incorporated into the Korean dances of the right in Bugaku and came under the general classification of Komagaku, by which name the music and dances of the right are known today.

On April 8, 752, the dedication ceremony for the gigantic statue of Rushana Buddha was held at the Todai-ji in Nara. It was a gala celebration attended by the reigning empress Koken and the retired emperor Shomu and his empress Komyo. The priest Bodhisena from India, now known as the high priest Baramon, was the master of ceremonies. Five thousand priests chanted sutras, and dances and songs from numerous countries of Asia were presented on a special stage built in front of the main sanctuary. It is stated in the *Todai-ji Chronicles* (Todai-ji Yoroku) that not only all the members of the imperial Gagaku-ryo—that is, the special Gagaku department—but also all the musicians and dancers trained by the priests Baramon and Fattriet at the Taian-ji, the Yakushi-ji, the Genko-ji, and the Kofuku-ji temples participated in the festivities. *Kume mai*, Togaku, Gigaku, and Komagaku were presented, along with numerous other types of song and dance.

Blending of Foreign and Domestic Styles

With the beginning of the Heian period in 794, contact with the Asian mainland began to decline, and the importation of song and dance styles from China, Korea, Bokkai, India, and Vietnam came to a halt. The following years were a time of assimilation and digestion of the large amounts of foreign culture that had been introduced into Japan during the preceding centuries. The less effective musical instruments were dropped from the orchestrations, and all music and dance was brought together under two major classifications: those of Togaku for compositions from China and of Komagaku for compositions from Manchuria and the Korean peninsula.

Emperor Kammu (reigned 781–806) built the new capital, called Heian-kyo (present Kyoto), according to the Chinese city-planning style, with the imperial palace in the north-central section and the whole city divided into two sections: the right and the left. There were a minister of the right and a minister of the left to represent the two sections, and court music was divided in a similar manner. Togaku became the music and dances of the left and Komagaku the music and dances of the right.

Previous to this time, musicians and dancers had been attached to temples and shrines, but the new court was extremely prosperous, and the aristocrats themselves developed an interest in learning to dance, to play musical instruments, and to compose songs and dances in Gagaku style. The famous eleventh-century novel *The Tale of Genji* tells of court life during this period, and one quickly discovers in its pages the great importance placed upon the arts in the daily life of the Heian-period nobility. Throughout this age, emperors and nobles composed pieces in honor of various court occasions and festivals, and these pieces are still performed today.

Shadows of Decline

The Heian period ended in a civil war between the rival clans of the Taira and the Minamoto, and the victory of the Minamoto in this conflict marked the beginning of the Kamakura period (1185–1333). Minamoto Yoritomo, the leader of the victorious forces, set up his shogunate capital at Kamakura, in eastern Japan, where he made the Tsurugaoka Hachiman

Shrine the center of his religious activities. In February 1191, at the invitation of Yoritomo, the Gagaku musician O no Yoshikata presented a performance of *kagura* at the shrine and then stayed on to serve there, teaching the music and dances of *kagura* to such generals as Hatakeyama Shigetada and Kajiwara Kagesue. In November 1193, Yoritomo rewarded Yoshikata for his services by presenting him with a fief.

Some years later, in 1233, Koma Chikazane, a Gagaku dancer from Nara, completed a ten-volume work on Gagaku called the *Kyokunsho*. This work contained information on all aspects of Gagaku as well as detailed explanations of the techniques for singing, dancing, and the playing of the musical instruments used in Gagaku.

During the century that followed, Gagaku was performed frequently, and various emperors and shoguns of the time were well known for their ability in playing the various Gagaku instruments. But the art itself had already become fixed, and its vitality began to decline.

During the brief interlude of the Kemmu Restoration (1334–36), when the emperor Godaigo attempted to restore imperial control over Japan, Gagaku seemed to regain some of its former glory, but by the beginning of the Muromachi period (1338–1573) it had once again gone into a sharp decline. When the Onin Rebellion broke out in 1467, Kyoto became a literal ghost town, and the imperial Gagaku department was dispersed.

Around this time Toyohara Sumiaki, an accomplished player of the *sho*, went into retirement and began to write the *Taigensho*. In this large set of books he set down a great bulk of knowledge concerning all aspects of Gagaku. In fact, without Sumiaki's work the art of Gagaku might have been completely lost. He completed the *Taigensho* in 1512.

The century or so of internal strife that followed the Onin Rebellion was brought to an end through the unifying efforts of Oda Nobunaga and Toyotomi Hideyoshi. Both of these military dictators had great respect for the imperial court (although they allowed it no political power) and gave it considerable support toward reconstruction after the ravages of a century of civil war. In 1588, for example, Hideyoshi entertained the emperor Goyozei for five days at his Jurakudai palace in Kyoto. On the first day of the emperor's visit, Hideyoshi presented a full *kangen* (orchestral) program of Gagaku music and, on the fourth day, a gala Bugaku program. The *kangen* numbers performed were *Gojoraku*, a *roei* piece, and *Gakka-en*. The Bugaku program included *Manzairaku, Engiraku, Taiheiraku, Komaboko, Ryo-o, Nasori, Saisoro, Kotoriso, Genjoraku*, and *Bato*.

Gagaku During the Edo Period

In 1603, five years after the death of Hideyoshi, Tokugawa Ieyasu assumed the title of shogun and established his capital at Edo (present Tokyo). This marked the beginning of the long age of Tokugawa rule known as the Edo, or Tokugawa, period (1603–1868). In 1615, with the fall of Osaka Castle to the Tokugawa forces and the slaughter of Hideyoshi's family, the Toyotomi line came to an end. During the peaceful two and a half centuries of the Edo period, Gagaku enjoyed a revival.

In 1626, when the third Tokugawa shogun, Iemitsu, visited Kyoto to demonstrate his power over the court as well as over all of Japan, he entertained the emperor Gomizuno-o for five days at Nijo Castle, a Tokugawa stronghold built to impress the citizenry of that city, which persisted in its loyalty to the court.

The entertainment for the emperor included a colorful array of *kangen* and Bugaku performances. On the *kangen* program was a revival of the *saibara* piece *Ise no Umi,* and the Bugaku program included a revival of *Seigaiha.*

Some years later, in 1642, performers were summoned from Kyoto, Osaka, and Nara to form a new Gagaku troupe associated with the Momijiyama mausoleum of Tokugawa Ieyasu inside the grounds of Edo Castle. This was the first time that a Gagaku troupe had been organized in eastern Japan, and its members were known as the "Momijiyama musicians."

The imperial court in Kyoto, held in strict subjection by the Tokugawa shogunate, went into a serious state of decline, and Gagaku performers found it most difficult to live on the extremely small salaries the court was forced to pay them. In 1666, the shogunate took the situation in hand and granted the fifty-one performers remaining at court a fief in Yamato Province (present Nara Prefecture) capable of producing 2,000 *koku* (about 10,000 bushels) of rice per year.

A system of examinations called the *kyudaie* was set up to ascertain each performer's level of ability and thereby to determine his share of the rice produced by the fief. The first *kyudaie* was carried out with a board of judges made up of eight leaders from the three Gagaku troupes of Kyoto, Nara, and Osaka. After that, the *kyudaie* was held every three years, and eight judges were chosen from each troupe, so that, for example, the performers from Kyoto were judged by a board of sixteen—a combined group of judges from Osaka and Nara. Ballots were cast on the basis of solo performances of five to seven pieces by each participating performer. Two ranks of proficiency were established—intermediate and advanced—and a performer was required to have eight affirmative votes to be awarded either of the ranks. Those who attained advanced rank were granted five *koku* of rice as an annual stipend, while those named to intermediate rank received three *koku*.

Aristocrats who had previously performed Gagaku only as a hobby began to study seriously and were allowed to take the examinations. Thus competition became intense. Rehearsal meetings were held regularly, and from thirty to fifty pieces a day were practiced during these sessions. Under this system the artistic ability of performers was brought to a level perhaps never before reached. The last *kyudaie* was held in 1865, three years before the collapse of the Tokugawa shogunate and the restoration of the emperor as head of state. Throughout the two hundred years during which these examinations were conducted, only six performers were granted the advanced rank by a unanimous vote of all sixteen judges on the examining board.

During these same two hundred years all the imperial festivals were revived one by one by the various emperors. Perhaps the most enthusiastic in this respect was Emperor Komei (reigned 1847–66), the last emperor of the Edo period. He was particularly well known for his virtuosity on the *wagon*. In March 1866 he performed three nights in a row for a special presentation of *mi-kagura*. Thus, when in December of the same year he retired to his quarters after playing only the first number at a *mi-kagura* performance, everyone present thought it most strange. Three days later, Emperor Komei died, depriving the world of Gagaku of its greatest patron and one of its most excellent performers during the Edo period.

CHAPTER 3

Gagaku in the Modern Age

Renovations and Reorganization

MORE THAN ONE HUNDRED YEARS have passed since the Meiji Restoration was carried out in 1868. On October 12 of that year, Emperor Meiji ascended the throne at the Shishin-den hall of the Imperial Palace in Kyoto. On December 26 of the same year he arrived at Edo Castle and set up his new residence there in the precinct called Nishinomaru. The city of Edo now became the new capital of Japan and was renamed Tokyo, and Japan itself entered the modern age. The Meiji government carried out reforms in every field, and Gagaku found itself once more in a most favorable position for rebirth and growth.

Reorganization of the teaching system and reforms in musical content were undertaken. These improvements were not as far-reaching as the great reforms in the music system of the early Heian period, but they were nevertheless of great significance in the modernization and revitalization of the art. As is evident from the public performances presented nowadays, it was at this point that Gagaku was brought out of the secrecy of the court and became available to the public.

The Gagaku Department was made a part of the cabinet on November 7, 1870, and the order was given that all court musicians were to be tested for ability and were to be further trained in the traditions of ancient music. The preservation and

133

teaching of important pieces was taken out of the hands of the imperial family and the court nobility who had held the positions of headmasters under the feudal-period system and was made the responsibility of four aristocratic families: the Fushimi, the Kikutei, the Hanazono, and the Saionji. Also, the secret *kagura* scores were placed in the custody of the Ayanokoji, the Yotsutsuji, and the Jimyoin families, and the order was given that all Gagaku performers must learn to perform *kagura*. At the same time, reforms in the examination system were ordered, together with a complete investigation and re-evaluation of all the Gagaku scores that had been in use up to that time. In addition to these innovations, the number of official court musicians was increased.

Previous to these changes, in 1869, the official Gagaku Rehearsal Hall was established in the Kojimachi district of Tokyo (a district adjoining the Imperial Palace grounds), where it remained until it burned down in the great earthquake of 1923, after which a new hall was built at the present location within the palace grounds. Also in 1869 a branch of the Gagaku Department was set up at the Gakushu-in (Peers' School) in Kyoto. Two years later it was moved to the grounds of the Kyoto Imperial Palace, and in 1877 it was closed.

The new spirit of the times, which stressed the equality of all levels of society, became manifest in a decree issued by the cabinet on May 27, 1873. It read in part: "In the past the learning of Gagaku has been limited to the aristocracy and official court musicians. In the future anyone who wishes may obtain permission to study it by simply applying at the Gagaku Rehearsal Hall. Bugaku lessons are also available." As a result, three men—Horikawa Morokatsu, Horiuchi Kigoro, and Omura Josaburo—not only took lessons in both *kagura* and Bugaku but also finally entered government service and became official members of the imperial Gagaku troupe. On the other hand, Togi Sueharu, a member of one of the traditional Gagaku families who entered the Gagaku school at the same time as these three, later left the troupe, took the name Tetsubue, and entered the Arts Association sponsored by the dramatist and critic Tsubouchi Shoyo. During the latter part of his life, Togi wrote *Studies of the History of Japanese Music*.

In December 1874 the order was given that all Gagaku musicians must take up the study of Western music. Somewhat over a year later, in March 1876, George William Fenton, an Englishman who had been hired as a teacher for the Navy Band, was given the post of music teacher in the Imperial Gagaku Department. Finally, on November 3, 1878, the first concert of Western music by court musicians was given at the Imperial Palace under the baton of Togi Suenaga.

In December of the same year a grand performance of *kangen*, Bugaku, and Western music was presented at the Gagaku Rehearsal Hall in the Imperial Palace grounds, and the general public was invited to attend. This was the first public performance given at this hall—the beginning of the regular Gagaku concerts that are presented there even today.

In 1879, court musicians Shiba Fujitsune, Togi Sueyoshi, Oku Yoshiisa, and Koshino Shuichi began taking piano lessons from Clara Matsuno, an Austrian kindergarten teacher resident in Japan. In the same year the Ministry of Education established a music research center to investigate and determine what music should be used in general education throughout the country's schools. Ue Sanemichi and Togi Takekata were appointed to represent the Imperial Gagaku Department in this new center.

The Gagaku Department system of ranks was reorganized in

1884, limiting the ranks to headmaster, assistant headmaster, instructor, musician, and apprentice. On March 9, 1894, a gala performance of *kangen* and Bugaku was presented in the Phoenix Room of the Imperial Palace in celebration of the twenty-fifth wedding anniversary of Emperor Meiji and Empress Shoken. The numbers on the program included *Manzairaku, Engiraku, Taiheiraku,* and *Bairo.*

During the Meiji era (1868–1912) the court musicians were extremely active in composing new pieces in Western style with Gagaku-type melodies. The best-known group of these pieces was called *Hoiku Shoka,* and one of them later became Japan's national anthem, *Kimi ga Yo.*

In 1917 a group of aristocrats formed a Gagaku troupe called the Itotake-kai, and the empress expressed her approval of their efforts by composing a song for them entitled *Itotake.* In 1921 the name of the Gagaku Department was changed to that of Department of Music. Around 1935 (to mention still another interesting facet of Gagaku history) Yamanoi Motokiyo and other Gagaku musicians produced a number of new compositions, including the *Minuet in the Hei Mode.*

The building that presently houses the Imperial Household Agency's Department of Music was completed on January 20, 1938. Shadows of approaching world war already overhung Japan, whose full-scale aggression against China had begun in 1937. From about 1940 on, most of the young Gagaku musicians were drafted into military service, and a great many of them went into other types of work after the war. Although the Department of Music was revived after the war, it suffered a considerable decrease in the number of musicians. Nevertheless, the value of Gagaku as a traditional art was officially recognized, and on May 12, 1955, the members of the Imperial Household

Agency's Gagaku troupe were designated by the Japanese government as Important Intangible Cultural Properties, or, as the more common expression has it, "living national treasures." And in the early summer of 1959 the troupe made a six-week performance tour of the United States.

Gagaku Throughout Japan Today

Mi-kagura was presented in 1889 at the Grand Shrine of Ise in celebration of the ritual reconstruction of the shrine buildings that is traditionally carried out every twenty years. The performers who participated in this ceremony decided to set up their own Gagaku troupe and invited an instructor from the Imperial Household Agency Gagaku troupe to assist in their training. At present the Ise Shrine troupe consists of seventeen performers of court-musician rank and three of apprentice rank. They participate in the various annual ceremonies held at the shrine.

The annual ceremonial Bugaku performance at the Atsuta Shrine in Nagoya, presented on the first of May, was revived in 1818 after long years of neglect. The present resident troupe, known as the Kiritake-kai, has fifty members. Also in Nagoya there are two active semi-amateur groups: the Bugaku Study Group and the Chubu Gagaku League. Members of these groups have written scholarly works on Gagaku, lectures are presented as part of the study program, and the two groups occasionally give joint performances.

Many valuable masks, costumes, musical instruments, and manuscripts concerning Gagaku are preserved at the Kasuga Shrine in Nara. At the Wakamiya Shrine, a smaller shrine within the precincts of the Kasuga Shrine, a festival called the On-matsuri is held annually on December 17. The Wakamiya Shrine was originally built in 1173, and the festival was first held in the same year. For this event, a special stage is set up in front of the ancient Yogo Pine, a tree associated in legend with the god of the shrine, who is said to have appeared under it at one time to perform a dance. Following the opening ceremony of the festival, *azuma asobi,* Yamato *mai,* and various Bugaku dances are performed. The resident troupe, known as the Kasuga Preservation Group, consists of about forty active members.

Gagaku is also performed at the Itsukushima Shrine on the island of Miyajima in the Inland Sea. The outdoor setting here is particularly impressive, for at high tide the shrine and its *torii* (ceremonial gate) seem to float on the water. Among the distinctive features of the shrine's famous "floating stage" are the holes drilled in the floor to serve as stands for the halberds used in such Bugaku dances as *Taiheiraku* and *Bairo.*

Troupes attached to the Kompira Shrine in Shikoku and the Tosho Shrine in Nikko (Tochigi Prefecture) perform *azuma asobi* at the grand festivals of these shrines. There are also Gagaku troupes at the Sapporo Shrine and the Otaru Sumiyoshi Shrine in Hokkaido and at the Mitsumine, Chichibu, and Hotozan shrines in Saitama Prefecture. In Chiba Prefecture there are such organizations as the Gagaku Doko-kai and others.

Kyoto, the traditional home of classical Japanese culture, has numerous Gagaku groups. These include the semi-amateur troupes called the Heian Gagaku-kai (fifty members), the Ga-in-kai (forty members), the Yaei Gagaku-kai (forty members), the Kyoto Bugaku-kai (made up mainly of women), and the Wagaku-kai. There is also an official Shrine Bureau troupe

98. Shunnoden *performed at National Theater, Tokyo*

99, *Kotokuraku performed at National Theater, Tokyo*

100. Genjoraku *performed at Atsuta Shrine*

102. Shunteika *performed at Shitenno-ji*

103. Embu *performed at Meiji Shrine*

104. *Painting:* Manzairaku *performed for Emperor Meiji's twenty-fifth wedding anniversary*

105. Hassen *performed at Kasuga Shrine*

106. Karyobin *performed at Ise Shrine*

108. Ayagiri *performed at Imperial Palace, Tokyo*

109. Ama *performed at Sumiyoshi Shrine*

110. Komaboko *performed at Kasuga Shrine*

111. Bairo *performed during imperial troupe's American tour*

112. Sonokoma *performed at United Nations General Assembly, New York*

113. Kishunraku *performed during imperial troupe's American tour*

114. *American girl receiving Bugaku instruction*

115. *Orchestral rehearsal at Ono Gagaku-kai, Tokyo*

116. *Bugaku practice at Nippon Bugaku-kai, Tokyo*

117. *Gagaku class, Tokyo University of Arts*

118. *Gagaku performance by Buddhist priests*

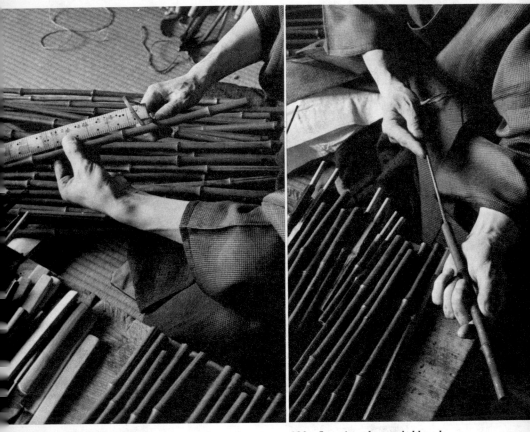

119. *Measuring bamboo pipes*

120. *Inserting plugs to hold reeds*

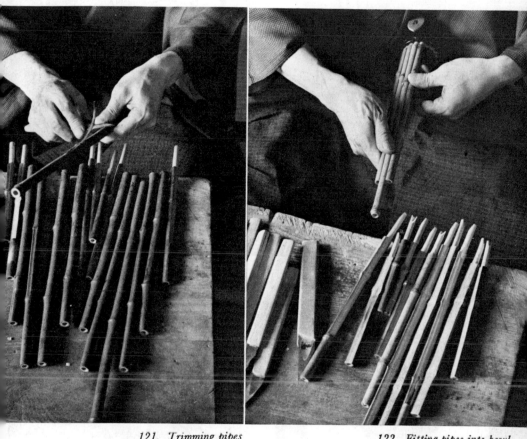

121. Trimming pipes

122. Fitting pipes into bowl

123. *Aligning pipes*

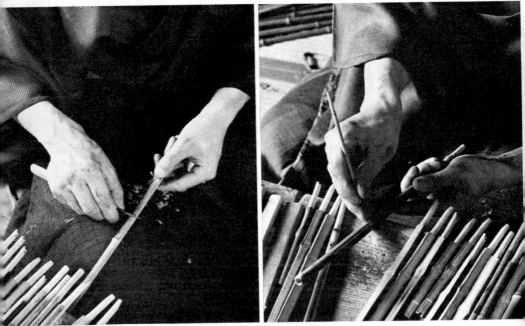

124. *Scraping pipes*

125. *Boring pitch holes*

126. *Marking finger holes*

127. *Applying lacquer glue*

128. *Cutting reeds from metal*

129. *Testing reeds for sound*

130. Painting reeds with nitrate of soda

131. Securing reeds to pipes

132. Setting reeds for tone

133. Testing pipes for pitch

134. *Testing finished* sho

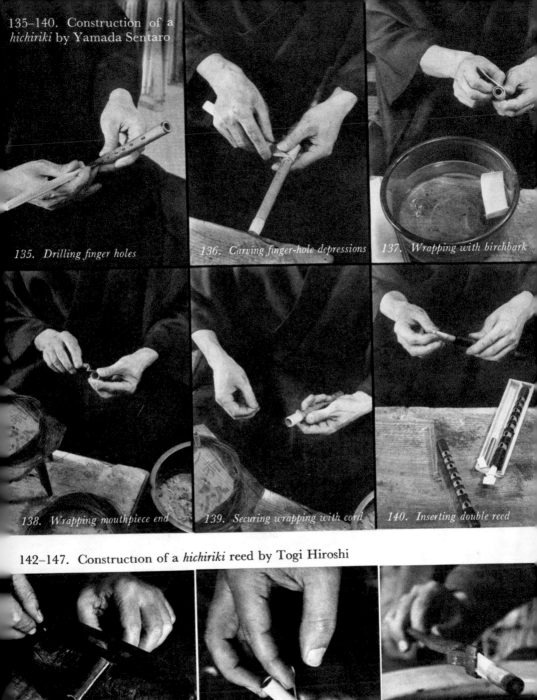

135–140. Construction of a *hichiriki* by Yamada Sentaro

135. *Drilling finger holes*

136. *Carving finger-hole depressions*

137. *Wrapping with birchbark*

138. *Wrapping mouthpiece end*

139. *Securing wrapping with cord*

140. *Inserting double reed*

142–147. Construction of a *hichiriki* reed by Togi Hiroshi

142. *Cutting reed from rush*

143. *Pasting paper over reed*

144. *Scorching insert end*

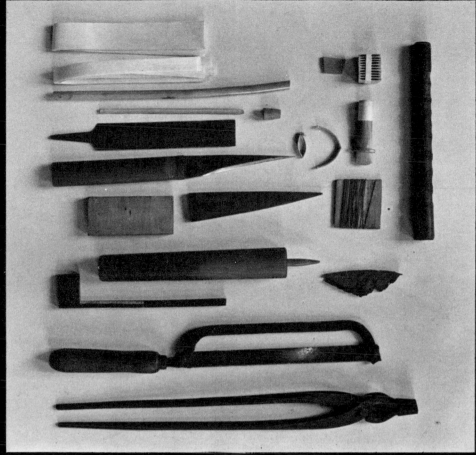

141. *Tools and materials for construction of* hichiriki

145. *Whittling insert end*

146. *Wrapping insert end*

147. *Cutting rattan for binding*

148–159. Construction of a flute by Kikuta Sokuho

148. *Selecting bamboo tube*

149. *Drilling finger holes*

150. *Cutting mouthpiece*

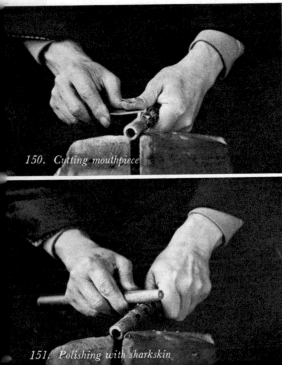

151. *Polishing with sharkskin*

152. *Lacquering mouthpiece end*

153. *Polishing inside with whetstone*

154. *Lacquering finger holes*

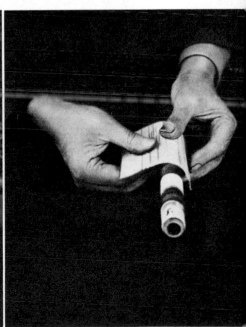

155. *Wrapping with cypress bark*

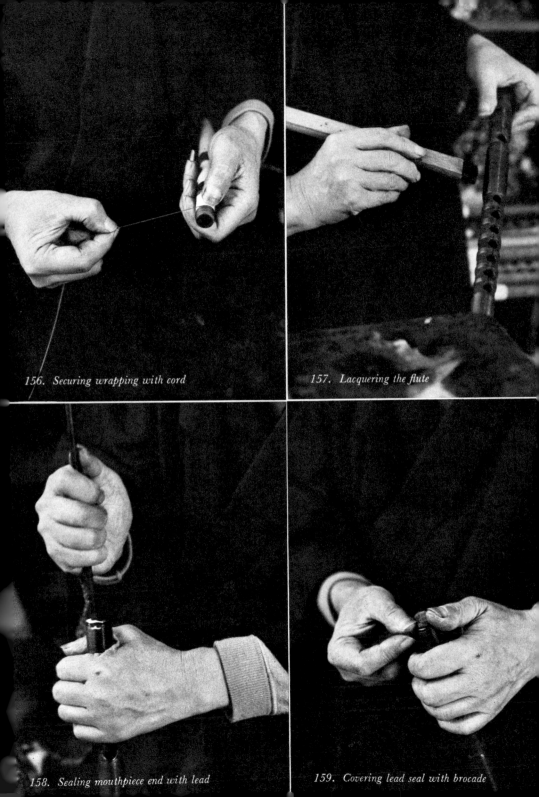

156. *Securing wrapping with cord*

157. *Lacquering the flute*

158. *Sealing mouthpiece end with lead*

159. *Covering lead seal with brocade*

160. *Ishimura Bunjiro repairing a biwa*

161. *Bugaku dancers dressing for performance*

162–169. Dancer Hayashi Tamio dresses for a performance

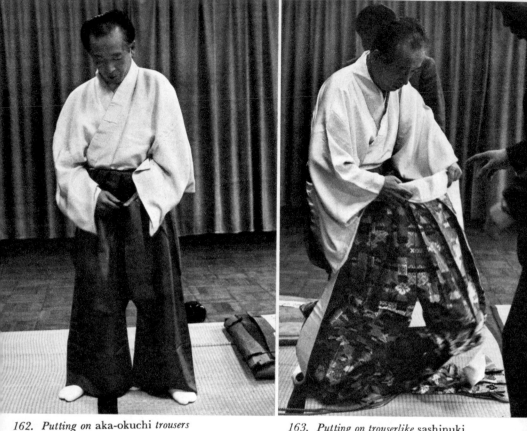

162. Putting on aka-okuchi *trousers*

163. Putting on trouserlike sashinuki

170–187. Paintings: Bugaku performers in dances of the left

170. Embu (dancer of the left)   *171. Shunnoden*   *172. Katen*

164. *Putting on cloaklike* ho

165. *Securing* ho *with sash*
series cont. ▷

173. Karyobin

174. Sogoko

175. Manjuraku

series cont. ▷

166. Putting on ryoto *breastplate*

167. Inspecting mask

176. Ryo-o

177. Ryo-o: *child's version*

178. Konju

168. *Putting on mask*   *169.* *Waiting for cue*

179. Bato   *180.* Hokuteiraku   *181.* Dagyuraku

series cont. ▷

188–199. Dance poses by Togi Hiroshi

188. Body erect; clenched hands at waist

189. Right arm and left foot extended forward

182. Ama

183. Kanshu

184. Shunteika

190. *Right arm to side; weight to left foot*   191. *Hands above shoulders; two fingers extended; knees bent*

series cont. ▷

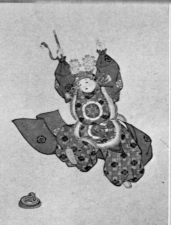

185. Sanju   186. Genjoraku: *child's version*   187. Saisoro

192. Hands clenched; arms raised; left foot forward   *193. Arms point to floor; right foot forward*

200–219. Paintings: Bugaku performers in dances of the right

200. Embu *(dancer of the right)*   *201.* Shokuha   *202.* Ayagiri

194. *Left arm extended; right hand at waist*

195. *Right arm back; left arm curved; weight on left foot*

series cont. ▷

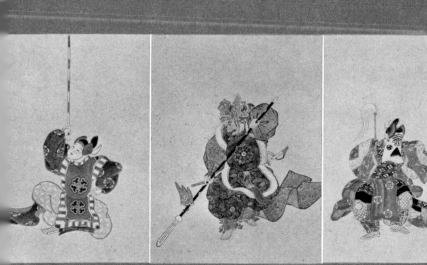

203. Komaboko

204. Kitoku

205. Soriko

series cont. ▷

196. *Right foot forward; right hand grasps trousers*   197. *Kneeling position, with head bowed and extended*

206. Shimmaka   207. Taisotoku   208. Kotokuraku

198. *Opening pose for* Sanju

199. *"Left dance" pose*

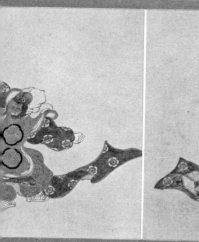

209. Nasori

210. Chikyu

211. Shinsotoku

series cont. ▷

新鳥蘇

212. Shintoriso

213. Kocho

214. Ringa

215. Hohin

216. Hassen

217. Rakuson: *child's version*

218. Onin

219. Ikkyoku

220. Azuma asobi

of thirty members which performs at the festivals and ceremonies of shrines and temples throughout the city. All these
organizations come together once a year to participate in a
recital sponsored by the Kyoto Gagaku Federation.

The Garyo-kai troupe was formed in Osaka in 1884. Today
it boasts a membership of more than sixty performers. This
troupe participates in all the ceremonies and festivals of Osaka's
Shitenno-ji temple. The stage at the Shitenno-ji is an impressive
stone structure built over a lotus pond. In June 1958 the Bugaku
costumes owned by the temple were designated as Important
Cultural Properties by the Japanese government. There are
also two independent Gagaku troupes in Osaka: the Koensha
and the Kansai Gagaku Matsukaze-kai.

In Tokyo both the Meiji Shrine and the Yasukuni Shrine
maintain their own Gagaku troupes to participate in their
various ceremonies and perform at their festivals. The Homei-
kai, the Ono Gagaku-kai, and the Kikuchi Gagaku-kai are
three Tokyo groups that were formed about the middle of the
Meiji era (around 1890) and are still active today. The Ono
Gagaku-kai has encouraged the composition and choreography
of new numbers by its members, who also publish their own
magazine, *Gagaku World*. The Gagaku Propagation Group, the
Gagaku Friends' Association, and the Gamci-kai were established in Tokyo around 1931. Recently, Oshida Yoshihisa,
one of the important members of the Gagaku Propagation
Group, broke away and founded the Japan Gagaku Group.

A number of Buddhist organizations in various parts of Japan
maintain their own Gagaku troupes. These include the troupes
of the Jodo-sect Zojo-ji temple, the Tsukiji Hongan-ji temple,
the Toyama branch of the Shingon sect, and the Sodo sect in
Tokyo; the troupe of the Jodo Shin sect in Ishikawa Prefecture;

the troupe of the Jodo-sect Komyo-ji temple in Kamakura; the troupe at the headquarters of the Tenri sect in Nara Prefecture; the troupe at the international headquarters of the Sango sect in Shimizu (Shizuoka Prefecture); and the troupe attached to the Rissho Kosei-kai.

The Academy of Oriental Music, headed by Tanabe Hisao, has for a long time conducted research on Gagaku as one phase of Oriental music. In recent years, among young scholars undertaking special research in the increasingly popular field of comparative music, there has been a tendency to look toward Gagaku as a subject for serious study. For this reason, both the Tokyo University of Arts and the National University of Music now offer regular courses of instruction in Gagaku and its techniques of performance.

A similar interest in Gagaku can be noted among modern Japanese composers, choreographers, and dancers, a number of whom have made use of its techniques and themes in their compositions. Moreover, Gagaku has attracted the attention of a number of Western musical scholars and composers, including the Americans Leo Traynor, Robert Garfias, and Alan Hovhaness; the German musician Eta Harich-Schneider (long resident in Japan); and the Israeli Uri Epstein—all of whom are experienced players of Gagaku instruments.

Posture of Musicians

Gagaku can be performed with the musicians standing in formation (*ritsugaku*), marching in formation (*michigaku*), or seated (*igaku*). There are two styles of seating: on stools and on the floor. Traditionally the round lacquered stool called a *shogi* was used, but recently Western-style chairs have come into favor and are widely used. When the musicians are seated on the floor, they assume the informal position with the legs crossed in front of the body rather than with the legs tucked under the body as in the formal Japanese style of sitting on the floor. The leg nearest the musician who holds the position of leader of the orchestra is always placed on top of the other leg. Old manuscripts of instructions state that the legs should be crossed as near the ankles as possible and that both knees should touch the floor. There are special instructions for the holding of the different instruments which bring about slight differences in the posture of the musician's body, but the point stressed throughout is that the body should maintain a comfortable position.

Dance Poses and Movement Patterns

The poses and gestures of Bugaku were originally literal, realistic movements, but over the long stretch of years they have become abstracted to the point where the choreography of Bugaku pieces today is made up of simple geometric patterns. In fact, the movements are so simple and refined that they require very little physical effort on the part of the dancer who performs them. In each dance there is a single movement motif around which the whole piece is built. This movement is the clue to the original meaning or "message" of the piece.

Movement and rhythm cues are taken from the beats of the large drum. Solo dances begin at center stage, and group dances—for the most part a series of solos—begin from the dancer's first position on the stage. The order of these solos is set according to the ranks of the dancers participating in the piece. Dance notation for Bugaku consists of simple directional marks and positions along with the names of the poses and movement sequences to be executed. An ancient book of Bugaku instructions picturesquely describes the ideal posture of the dancer as being "like tinted leaves blown about in a storm on a mountain in autumn" for the dances of the left and "like a willow waving in the spring breeze" for the dances of the right.

Postscript

In this book I have attempted to give a brief outline of the form and quality of Gagaku and its history. I would like to be able to go on to discuss the position and meaning of Gagaku in present-day Japanese society as well as its future possibilities, for, like the hunter in the old Japanese proverb who "chases the deer and forgets about the mountain," we who spend our lives rehearsing and performing Gagaku tend to lose sight of its broader significance and its relationship to the outside world. In any event, I hope I have conveyed to my readers at least some of the feeling and flavor of this ancient performing art.

If I may add a word of personal emotional opinion in closing, I wish to express my strong feeling that the public performances of Bugaku and *kangen* today are of such a level that they permit the audience to gain a complete appreciation of the infinitely placid, crystalline beauty of Gagaku. I hope that the existence of Gagaku will continue not only to provide interludes of quiet diversion for those who attend the performances but also to give them something of enduring value to enhance the pleasure of their daily lives.

Chronology

Legendary period	The evolution of the important imperial ceremonial songs and dances called *mi-kagura* began. Emperor Jimmu (supposedly reigned 660–585 B.C.) originated the *kume mai*.
A.D. 453	Eighty musicians were sent from the Korean kingdom of Shiragi (Silla) to participate in the funeral of Emperor Ingyo.
531–39	*Azuma asobi* was originated during the reigns of the emperors Ankan and Senka.
554	Four musicians were sent from the Korean kingdom of Kudara (Paekche) as replacements for an equal number who had previously been sent at an earlier date.
560–71	Buddhism was introduced into Japan around this time.
593	Beginning of regency of Prince Shotoku (572–622), who worked to spread Buddhism and its ritual music. During this year the Shitenno-ji temple was built in Osaka, and a music department was set up there by Prince Shotoku.
612	Mimashi, a musician from the Korean kingdom of Kudara (Paekche) who had studied in China, migrated to Japan, where he became a Japanese citizen and taught Gigaku.
645	Togaku (Chinese music) was introduced into Japan during the Taika Reform.
673–86	Reign of Emperor Temmu, who originated the *gosechi-no-mai*.
684	Komagaku (Korean music) was performed at the Japanese imperial court.
693	Empress Jito sponsored a performance of the Chinese song-and-dance form called *toka* for the New Year's celebration.
701	A music department called the Gagaku-ryo was set up at the imperial court in compliance with laws promulgated by Emperor Mommu.
702	*Gotei Taiheiraku*, a Togaku piece, was performed at a New Year's banquet for government officials.

191

704   The ambassador Awata no Mahito returned from China with the Togaku piece *Odaiha Jinraku.*

710   The capital of Japan was moved to Nara, and the Nara period (710–84) began.

713   The kingdom known to the Japanese as Bokkai was established around this time in what is now Manchuria.

727   An ambassador from Bokkai came to visit the court of Emperor Shomu, and relations were established between this kingdom and Japan.

731   A revision of personnel in the Gagaku-ryo increased the number of those specializing in foreign music and decreased the number specializing in traditional Japanese music.

735   The ambassador Kibi no Mabi returned from China with gifts that included musical instruments and a ten-volume work entitled *A Digest of Musical Matters* (Gakusho Yoroku).

736   The priests Bodhisena (in Japanese, Baramon) from India and Fattriet (in Japanese, Buttetsu) from Vietnam arrived in Japan and began the teaching of eight famous Gagaku pieces to musicians and dancers at the Taian-ji in Nara and the Shitenno-ji in Osaka.

740   Emissaries from the kingdom of Bokkai performed music of their country at the Japanese court.

743   Emperor Shomu composed a dance in the *gosechi-no-mai* style. The crown prince took part in a dance performance.

746   More than one thousand people emigrated from Bokkai to Japan.

749   Foreign music and dance were performed along with *gosechi-no-mai, ta mai, kume mai,* and other native forms.

752   Musicians and dancers from the Gagaku-ryo and from various temples performed at the dedication ceremony for the statue of Rushana Buddha at the Todai-ji, in Nara. Members of the imperial family and the court nobility also took part in the festivities by performing *gosechi-no-mai, kume mai,* and *toka.*

794   The capital was moved to Heian-kyo (present Kyoto), and the Heian period (794–1185) began.

805   A nationwide epidemic forced a reduction in the number of Gagaku performers.

807   The famous *biwa* player Fujiwara Sadatoshi was born.

809   The Gagaku-ryo underwent a reduction in personnel. During this same year a teacher of Southeast Asian music was added to its staff.

810	During the Konin era, which began with this year and ended in 823, Gagaku was made an official function of the court. At the same time, the Outa-dokoro was established for the study and performance of traditional Japanese music and dance, while the Gagaku-ryo was made responsible for the study of foreign music and dance alone.
833	From about this time, foreign music began to be divided into the two classifications of Togaku and Komagaku.
839	Fujiwara Sadatoshi returned from T'ang China with a collection of *biwa* music.
861	Togaku and Komagaku were performed along with Yamato *mai* and other native Japanese forms of music and dance at the Todai-ji in Nara.
867	Fujiwara Sadatoshi died at the age of sixty.
874	At the grand festival of the Jogan-ji, musicians and dancers from the Gagaku-ryo, the Taian-ji, and the Kofuku-ji performed Togaku, Komagaku, and other types of foreign and native music. From about this year on, some forty young imperial princes and court noblemen became dancers, and their performances were attended by members of the imperial family, the court nobility, and all government officials.
920	*Azuma asobi* was established as part of the Gagaku repertoire by imperial decree.
942	*Azuma asobi* was performed at the Gion Shrine in Kyoto.
948	Around this time a government office of music known as the Gaku-dokoro was established in addition to the Gagaku-ryo.
1002	*Mi-kagura* was performed in the Naishi-dokoro, the hall in the imperial palace where the sacred mirror was venerated. From this time on, it was performed in alternate years.
1007	*The Tale of Genji*, Murasaki Shikibu's celebrated novel of court life, was probably completed around this time.
1008	The first mention of the song form known as *imayo* is found in an entry in the *Murasaki Shikibu Nikki* (Diary of Murasaki Shikibu) for this year.
1016	*Mi-kagura* was performed in the Seishodo, a hall in the imperial palace reserved for ceremonial music and dances.
1174	Thirty talented performers of the song form called *imayo* engaged in a two-week competition at the palace of the retired emperor Goshirakawa.
1185	The Heian period came to a close with the total defeat of the

	Taira forces in their war against the Minamoto. The Kamakura period (1185–1333) began.
1191	Minamoto Yoritomo invited the Gagaku musician O no Yoshikata to present a performance of *kagura* at the Tsurugaoka Hachiman Shrine in Kamakura.
1192	Minamoto Yoritomo became shogun and established his government at Kamakura.
1233	The Gagaku dancer Koma Chikazane completed the *Kyokunsho*, a ten-volume work on Gagaku.
1334–36	Interlude of the Kemmu Restoration, when Emperor Godaigo attempted to restore imperial control over Japan. Gagaku was revived after a long period of neglect.
1338	Ashikaga Takauji was appointed shogun, and the Muromachi period (1338–1573) began.
1467	The Onin Rebellion broke out and continued until 1477. In this conflict the city of Kyoto was devastated, and the imperial Gagaku department was dispersed.
1512	The retired Gagaku musician Toyohara Sumiaki completed the *Taigensho*, a large compendium of knowledge concerning all aspects of Gagaku.
late 16th century	The military dictators Oda Nobunaga and Toyotomi Hideyoshi succeeded in unifying the country after a century or so of civil strife. The Momoyama period (1573–1602) witnessed a revival and new flowering of the arts.
1588	Hideyoshi invited Emperor Goyozei to his Jurakudai palace in Kyoto for a five-day entertainment that included *kangen* and Bugaku.
1603	Tokugawa Ieyasu assumed the title of shogun and established his capital at Edo (present Tokyo). The Edo period (1603–1868) began, and Gagaku enjoyed a new revival, both in Edo and in Kyoto.
1626	Tokugawa Iemitsu, the third shogun, entertained Emperor Gomizuno-o for five days at Nijo Castle, the Tokugawa stronghold in Kyoto. The diversions included *kangen* and Bugaku performances.
1642	The Gagaku troupe known as the "Momijiyama musicians" was formed at Edo Castle.
1666	The shogunate granted a 2,000-*koku* fief to the Gagaku musicians and set up a system of examinations called the *kyudaie*.
1753	The Outa-dokoro was revived at the imperial court.
1813	*Azuma asobi* was revived.

1818   *Kume mai* was revived.

1847–66   Reign of Emperor Komei, the most enthusiastic participant in the revival of the Imperial festivals.

1866   Emperor Komei died.

1868   The Meiji Restoration was carried out.

1869   The official Gagaku Rehearsal Hall was established in Tokyo.

1870   The Gagaku Department was made a part of the cabinet, and numerous reforms were made in the teaching and preservation of Gagaku.

1873   Instruction in Gagaku and Bugaku was made available to the general public by cabinet decree.

1874   Gagaku musicians were ordered to take up the study of Western music.

1876   The Englishman George William Fenton was given the post of music teacher in the Imperial Gagaku Department.

1878   The first concert of Western music by court musicians was given at the Imperial Palace in Tokyo. The first public performance by court musicians was given at the Gagaku Rehearsal Hall.

1879   Gagaku musicians began taking piano lessons. The Ministry of Education established a music research center at which the Imperial Gagaku Department was represented.

1884   The Gagaku Department system of ranks was reorganized.

1894   A gala performance of *kangen* and Bugaku was presented in honor of the twenty-fifth wedding anniversary of Emperor Meiji and Empress Shoken. The Sino-Japanese War of 1894–95 began.

1904   The Russo-Japanese War of 1904–5 began.

1917   A group of aristocrats formed the Gagaku troupe called the Itotake-kai.

1921   The name of the Gagaku Department was changed to that of Department of Music.

1935   Around this time Yamanoi Motokiyo and other Gagaku musicians produced a number of new compositions, including the *Minuet in the Hei Mode.*

1937–45   Japan was at war in China and, from 1941, in the Pacific. During this period most of the young Gagaku musicians were drafted into military service, and many turned to other occupations after the war.

1938   The building that presently houses the Imperial Household Agency's Department of Music was completed.

1955   The members of the Imperial Household Agency's Gagaku troupe were designated by the Japanese government as Important Intangible Cultural Properties.

1959   The imperial Gagaku troupe made a six-week performance tour of the United States.

1967   The imperial Gagaku troupe made its first appearance at the new National Theater in Tokyo, performing *Shunnoden, Manjuraku,* and *Onintei.*

Commentaries on the Illustrations

1. *Bato:* a dance of the left introduced from Southeast Asia during the eighth century. Gagaku theater, Imperial Palace, Tokyo.

2. Gagaku orchestra performing at the theater in the Imperial Palace compound, Tokyo. In the background at left is the great drum of the left; at left of center, the *tsuridaiko* (suspended drum).

3. *Nasori:* a dance of the right in the *hashiri mai* (running dance) classification. The dancers represent two fierce dragons frolicking and enjoying each other's company. Gagaku theater, Imperial Palace, Tokyo.

4. *Manzairaku:* a dance of the left in the *bun no mai* (literary dance) classification. The dancers represent phoenixes, and the dance is based on an ancient Chinese legend. Gagaku theater, Imperial Palace, Tokyo.

5. *Bairo:* a dance of the right in the *bu no mai* (warrior dance) classification. The dancers are accoutred with swords, shields, and lances

(here seen on floor of stage). Gagaku theater, Imperial Palace, Tokyo.

6. *Engiraku:* a dance of the right in the *bun no mai* (literary dance) classification. It takes its name from the Engi era (901–22), during which it was first presented. Gagaku theater, Imperial Palace, Tokyo.

7. Yamato *mai:* an ancient native Japanese dance from the Yamato district (present Nara Prefecture). It is performed every year at the Imperial Palace on the evening before the harvest festival in November. Gagaku theater, Imperial Palace, Tokyo.

8. *Ryo-o* (or *Ranryo-o*): a dance of the left in the *hashiri mai* (running dance) classification. The dancer, wearing a mask surmounted by a fabulous bird, portrays a victorious king in an ancient legend. (See also Plates 43 and 101.) Gagaku theater, Imperial Palace, Tokyo.

9. Bugaku performance at the theater in the Imperial Palace compound, Tokyo. The theater is main-

197

tained by the Imperial Household Agency's Department of Music.

10. *Gojoraku:* a dance of the left designed to express the five Confucian virtues. Gagaku theater, Imperial Palace, Tokyo.

11. *Konju:* a dance of the left portraying the antics of a drunken "barbarian." Gagaku theater, Imperial Palace, Tokyo.

12. Gagaku orchestra accompanying a Bugaku dance at the theater in the Imperial Palace compound, Tokyo. For purely orchestral numbers, the musicians occupy the main stage in the foreground.

13. *Hichiriki:* a short double-reed wind instrument of ancient West Asian origin. The construction of the body is quite similar to that of a flute.

14. *Sho:* a type of mouth organ made up of seventeen bamboo pipes. Usually five or six pipes are sounded together in a prolonged chord.

15. *Oteki:* a transverse bamboo flute with seven stops. It has the alternate names of *ryuteki* and *omobue.*

16. *San no tsuzumi:* an hourglass-shaped drum of Korean origin. It is played with only one stick.

17. *Dadaiko:* one of two huge drums that stand at left and right in the upstage corners of the Gagaku stage. This one is known as the great drum of the left, while the other is called the great drum of the right.

18. Dance properties: a lance and a shield for the warrior dance *Bairo.* (See also Plate 5.)

19. *Shoko:* a suspended brass gong sounded with two hard-tipped sticks.

20. *Tsuri-daiko:* a suspended drum played with two sticks—the most commonly used drum in Gagaku.

21. *Kakko:* a small horizontal drum with two lashed heads. It is played with two sticks and, being of Chinese origin, is used in Togaku.

22. Musicians in costume for an orchestral performance at the Gagaku theater of the Imperial Palace, Tokyo.

23. *So* (or *gakuso*): a zitherlike thirteen-stringed instrument of Chinese origin—predecessor of the *koto.* (See also Plate 25.)

24. *Biwa:* a pear-shaped lute with four strings and four frets, played with a small plectrum (*bachi*). The *biwa* originated in Central Asia and reached Japan by way of China.

25. Finger picks for the *so.* (See also Plate 23.)

26. Wind instruments. From left to right: *sho, hichiriki, kagurabue, oteki,* and *komabue.*

27. Dance score for *Manzairaku,* a dance of the left.

28. Score for *roei,* an ancient type of of native Japanese vocal music.

29. Halberds and lances used in *bu no mai* (warrior dances).

30. Helmet for *Sogoko,* a dance of the left. (See Plate 174 and commentary.)

31. *Ryoto:* a type of decorative breastplate worn by the dancer in *Ryo-o.* The dance itself is shown in Plates 8 and 101.

32. Dancer's hard lacquered hat with curled top piece (left) and chin cord with tassels (right). The hat is worn in such dances as *Bairo* (Plate 5) and *Gojoraku* (Plate 10).

33. Dancer's Chinese-style hat.

34. *Ho:* overgarment for the dance *Seigaiha.* The design pictures plovers against a background of stylized ocean waves.

35. *Hassen* mask. The mask and headdress represent the head of a crane with a greatly shortened bill, while the jingling of the silver bell suspended from the mouth suggests the bird's cry. The dance itself is pictured in Plates 105 and 216.

36. *Nasori* mask. This blue mask with silver fangs represents a dragon. The dance in which it is worn is pictured in Plate 3.

37. *Genjoraku* mask. The solo dancer in *Genjoraku* (Plate 100), who portrays a mythical Indian king, wears this intricately carved flame-colored mask.

38. *Somakusha* mask. *Somakusha* is a dance of the left in which a solo dancer represents a joyous mountain god.

39. *Saisoro* mask. This mask is worn by the solo dancer in *Saisoro* (Plate 187), who portrays an old man.

40. *Kitoku* mask. The solo dancer in *Kitoku,* a warrior dance of the right (Plate 204), wears this mask and accompanying helmet.

41. *Zomen:* general-purpose mask used in various dances. (See Plate 109.)

42. *Kotokuraku* mask. This mask with a movable nose is used in the group dance *Kotokuraku* (Plate 99).

43. *Ryo-o* (or *Ranryo-o*) mask owned by the Iwashimizu Hachiman Shrine, Kyoto. (See also Plate 8 and commentary and Plate 101.)

44. Five-stringed *biwa* of the Nara period (710-84). Red sandalwood decorated with mother-of-pearl. Shoso-in, Nara.

45. Detail from *Bugaku,* a pair of two-panel screens by Tawaraya Sotatsu (early seventeenth century). The dances depicted are *Genjoraku* (above) and *Ryo-o* (below). Sambo-in, Kyoto. Designated as an Important Cultural Property.

46. *Kangen* (orchestral music) recital by women of the medieval court. Detail from a picture scroll entitled *The Tale of Princess Joruri.* Atami Art Museum, Shizuoka Prefecture.

47, 48. Twelve-panel folding screen by To-o picturing various Bugaku dances.

49-51. Details from an illustrated

chronicle of events in the life of Emperor Komei (1831-66). 49: Gagaku orchestral performance at the Kyoto Imperial Palace, 1861, in celebration of the emperor's first appearance as a *sho* player. 50: *Mi-kagura* performance at the Kyoto Imperial Palace, 1866—the last performance in which the emperor participated. 51: *Kume mai* performance at the Kyoto Imperial Palace in celebration of the emperor's coronation in 1847. The scroll is owned by the Imperial Household Agency, Tokyo.

52. Mask of Bonten (Brahma) used in the ancient dramatic procession called *gyodo*. Tokyo National Museum.

53. Detail of an octagonal bronze lantern showing a Buddhist angel-musician. Nara period (710–84). Todai-ji, Nara.

54–57. Musical instruments of the Nara period (710–84) preserved in the Shoso-in repository. 54: Carved *shakuhachi* (bamboo flute), with detail of lower side shown at left and upper side shown at right. 55: Birch-wrapped *shakuhachi*, with upper side shown at left and lower side shown at right. 56: Black-lacquered *sho* (bamboo mouth organ). 57: *Sho* made of Chinese bamboo. Shoso-in, Nara.

58–61. Masks used in Gigaku, an ancient but now extinct form of Buddhist ritual drama. 58: Rikishi, a Buddhist demigod. 59: Gojo (literally, "Chinese woman"). 60: Goko (literally, "Chinese prince"). 61: Karura (Garuda), a mythological bird. The masks in Plates 58 and 59 are in the Shoso-in, Nara; those in Plates 60 and 61 are owned by the Japanese government.

62. Bugaku mask for *Sanju*, a warrior dance of the left. Kasuga Shrine, Nara. The dance itself is pictured in Plate 185.

63. Bugaku mask for *Bato*, a solo dance of the left portraying a son's revenge against a beast that has killed his father. Itsukushima Shrine, Hiroshima Prefecture. The dance itself is shown in Plates 1 and 179.

64. Bugaku mask for *Onintei*. Owned by the Tamukeyama Shrine, Nara, and classed as an Important Cultural Property.

65. Bugaku mask for *Ama Ni no Mai*. Owned by the Atsuta Shrine, Nagoya, and classed as an Important Cultural Property.

66–69. Stone relief carvings of Buddhist angels as Gigaku musicians. Cave 3, Kung-hsien, Honan Province, China.

70. Copy of a wall painting showing celestial musicians in the Western Paradise of Amida Buddha. Cave 172, Tun-huang, Kansu Province, China.

71, 72. Sections of musical notation for the five-stringed *koto*. Owned by the Yomei Bunko, Kyoto, and designated as a National Treasure.

73. Secret musical notation for the *kagura wagon* (an early form of the *koto*) said to be in the handwriting of Fujiwara Michinaga (966–1027). Owned by the Konoe family.

74–77. Paintings of dancers and musicians. 74. *Dagyuraku,* a dance of the left. 75. Tent for musicians of the left. 76. *Komaboko,* a dance of the right. 77. Tent for musicians of the right. Owned by the Imperial Household Agency, Tokyo.

78. Court ladies of the Heian period (794–1185) playing musical instruments. Detail from the *Tale of Genji* picture scroll (twelfth century). Owned by the Tokugawa Reimeikai, Tokyo, and designated as a National Treasure.

79. Dancers and musicians performing *Karyobin,* a dance of the left. Detail from a picture scroll showing dances of the twelfth century. Owned by the Tokyo University of Arts. (See also Plates 106 and 173.)

80. *Azuma asobi:* an ancient type of native Japanese music and dance in Shinto rituals. Detail from the picture scroll *Kasuga Gongen Reigen Ki* (early fourteenth century), which deals with miracles attributed to the deity of the Kasuga Shrine, Nara. Imperial Household Collection, Tokyo.

81. *Taiheiraku:* a warrior dance of the left. Detail from the fifteenth-century picture scroll *Ippen Shonin Eden* (Pictorial Biography of Saint Ippen). Owned by the Maeda Ikutoku-kai, Tokyo, and classed as an Important Cultural Property.

82. Antique *kagura* score reconstructed by the nineteenth-century Gagaku musician Abe Sueharu. Owned by Abe Isao.

83. Old record of Gagaku traditions and training methods. Owned by the author.

84. Detail from score of the orchestral piece *Etenraku* in the handwriting of Emperor Goyozei (1571–1617). Owned by the Fushimi Inari Shrine, Kyoto.

85. Section from an old list of official ranks among employees of the court. Gagaku musicians and dancers are named among such other personnel as astronomers, tutors, paymasters, and chefs. Owned by the Toyo Bunko, Tokyo.

86. Beginning of preface to *Taigensho,* a chronicle of Gagaku history and customs written by Toyohara Sumiaki in the early sixteenth century. Owned by the Imperial Household Agency, Tokyo.

87–95. Scenes from two pictorial records portraying regular and special performances of Gagaku. The two records are the *Korei Koji no Zu* (Pictures of Regular Court Ceremonies; Plates 87, 89–94) and the *Rinji Koji no Zu* (Pictures of Special Court Ceremonies; Plates 88, 95). Both records are owned by the Imperial Household Agency, Tokyo.

87. *Embu* (a congratulatory halberd dance) performed for the emperor in the south garden of the Kyoto Imperial Palace.

88. Gagaku performance at the Kyoto Imperial Palace for "envoys from the east"—that is, representatives of the shogunate government.

89. Female dancers performing for the Festival of the White Horse, a part of the New Year's celebrations at the Kyoto Imperial Palace.

90. Gagaku performance as part of the New Year's celebrations at the Kyoto Imperial Palace.

91. Bugaku dancers on horseback at the Kitano Shrine Festival in Kyoto.

92. *Mi-kagura* performance at the Kamo Shrine, Kyoto.

93. Bugaku performance at the Kamo Shrine, Kyoto.

94. Springtime performance of Gagaku at the Kyoto Imperial Palace.

95. Dances of native Japanese origin performed at the Kyoto Imperial Palace in celebration of the enthronement of a new emperor.

96. Gagaku performance at a religious ceremony in the Kyoto Imperial Palace. Detail from an illustrated chronicle of events in the life of Emperor Komei (1831–66). Owned by the Imperial Household Agency, Tokyo.

97. Antique woodblock print picturing Gagaku musicians and a dancer.

98. *Shunnoden,* a dance of the left, performed by the imperial Gagaku troupe at the National Theater, Tokyo.

99. *Kotokuraku,* a dance of the right, performed by the imperial Gagaku troupe at the National Theater, Tokyo.

100. *Genjoraku,* a dance of the left, performed by a member of the Kiritake-kai troupe at the Atsuta Shrine, Nagoya. The dancer portrays a mythical Indian king who triumphs over a malevolent serpent.

101. *Ryo-o* (or *Ranryo-o*), a dance of the left, performed at the Itsukushima Shrine, Hiroshima Prefecture. (See also Plate 8 and commentary.)

102. *Shunteika,* a dance of the left, performed by members of the Gaku-ryo-kai troupe at the Shitenno-ji temple, Osaka.

103. *Embu* dancer of the left in a Gagaku performance at the Meiji Shrine, Tokyo.

104. Painting: *Manzairaku,* a dance of the left, performed at the Tokyo Imperial Palace in celebration of Emperor Meiji's twenty-fifth wedding anniversary. Owned by the Seitoku Kinen Kaigakan, Tokyo.

105. *Hassen,* a dance of the right, performed by members of the Kogaku Hozon-kai troupe at the Kasuga

Shrine, Nara. (See also Plate 35 and commentary.)

106. *Karyobin,* a dance of the left, performed in the Kagura Hall of the Ise Shrine, Mie Prefecture. (See also Plates 79 and 173.)

107. Performance of *azuma asobi* by members of the Heian Gagaku-kai troupe at the Shimo Kamo Shrine, Kyoto. Photograph from the collection of Oshida Yoshihisa.

108. *Ayagiri,* a dance of the right, performed by members of the imperial Gagaku troupe at the theater in the Imperial Palace compound, Tokyo.

109. *Ama,* a dance of the left, performed by members of the Gakuryo-kai troupe at the Sumiyoshi Shrine, Osaka.

110. *Komaboko,* a dance of the right, performed by members of the Kogaku Hozon-kai troupe at the Kasuga Shrine, Nara.

111. *Bairo,* a dance of the right, performed by members of the imperial Gagaku troupe during their American tour in 1959. (See also Plate 5.)

112. *Sonokoma,* a *kagura* number, performed by members of the imperial Gagaku troupe at the United Nations General Assembly, New York, 1959.

113. *Kishunraku,* a dance of the left, performed by members of the imperial Gagaku troupe during their American tour in 1959.

114. An American girl receiving instruction in Bugaku at the Ono Gagaku-kai, Tokyo.

115. *Kangen* (orchestral music) rehearsal at the Ono Gagaku-kai, Tokyo.

116. Bugaku practice at the Nippon Bugaku-kai, Tokyo.

117. Gagaku class, Department of Music, Tokyo University of Arts.

118. Gagaku performance by Buddhist priests at the Kannon-ji temple, Ichikawa City, Chiba Prefecture. The performers are members of a Shingon-sect Gagaku troupe.

119–134. Construction of a *sho* (bamboo mouth organ) by Yamada Sentaro, Kyoto.

119. Bamboo pipes are measured to determine proper lengths for different tones.

120. Plugs are inserted in the pipes for holding the reeds.

121. The pipes are roughly trimmed so that they will fit compactly together in a cluster.

122. The pipes are fitted into the bowl of the *sho.*

123. The pipes are examined for proper alignment.

124. The outer skin of the bamboo is scraped off.

125. Pitch holes are bored in the pipes.

126. Finger holes are marked.

127. Lacquer glue is applied to ends of pipes before insertion of reeds.

128. Reeds are cut from metal sheets.

129. The reeds are tested by ear.

130. Each reed is painted with nitrate of soda to prevent leakage of air.

131. The reeds are secured at the ends of the bamboo pipes.

132. Each reed is set for tone.

133. The pipes are tested for pitch.

134. The finished *sho* is tested.

135–140. Construction of a *hichiriki* (double-reed flutelike instrument) by Yamada Sentaro, Kyoto.

135. Finger holes are drilled in the bamboo tube.

136. Depressions are carved out around the finger holes.

137. The first layer of white birchbark covering is put in place.

138. White birchbark is wrapped around the mouthpiece end.

139. The birchbark wrapping is secured in place with special cord.

140. The double reed is inserted to complete the *hichiriki*.

141. Tools and materials for the construction of the *hichiriki*.

142–147. Construction of a *hichiriki* reed by Togi Hiroshi, Department of Music, Imperial Household Agency, Tokyo.

142. Section is cut from a special type of rush to form the reed.

143. After the outer skin has been peeled off, paper is pasted over the mouthpiece end.

144. The insert end of the reed is slightly scorched over glowing charcoal.

145. The insert end of the reed is whittled to proper diameter.

146. The insert end of the reed is wrapped with special paper.

147. Rattan is cut for binding the reed.

148–159. Construction of a flute by Kikuta Sokuho, Nagoya.

148. A bamboo tube is selected and measured.

149. The finger holes are drilled.

150. The mouthpiece is cut.

151. The surface of the bamboo tube is polished with sharkskin.

152. Lacquer is applied at the mouthpiece end.

153. The inside of the flute is polished with a whetstone.

154. Lacquer is applied around the finger holes.

155. Thin sheets of cypress bark are wrapped around the flute.

156. The bark is secured in place with special cord.

157. The whole flute is lacquered.

158. The mouthpiece end of the flute is sealed with lead.

159. The lead seal is covered with brocade.

160. Ishimura Bunjiro, of the Imperial Household Agency's Department of Music, begins repair work on a *biwa* (lute).

161. Bugaku dancers dressing for a performance at the theater in the Imperial Palace compound, Tokyo.

162–169. Bugaku dancer Hayashi Tamio, of the imperial Gagaku troupe, dresses for a performance.

162. The solid-red trousers called *aka-okuchi* are put on over a basic white kimono.

163. The *sashinuki,* a trouserlike garment made of brocade, is put on over the *aka-okuchi* and tied in place with a white sash.

164. The dancer next dons the *ho,* a cloaklike outer garment with wide sleeves.

165. The *ho* is secured in place with a sash.

166. The *ryoto,* an embroidered breastplate, is put on and secured with a heavy silk cord.

167. The mask is inspected.

168. The mask is put on and tied in place.

169. The costumed dancer awaits his cue.

170–187. Paintings of Bugaku performers in dances of the left. Owned by the Department of Music, Imperial Household Agency, Tokyo.

170. *Embu:* a congratulatory halberd dance performed by one dancer of the left (shown here) and one dancer of the right. (See also Plates 103 and 200.)

171. *Shunnoden.* (See also Plate 98.)

172. *Katen:* a dance performed by either four or six dancers.

173. *Karyobin.* (See also Plates 79 and 106.)

174. *Sogoko:* a dance of Indian origin transmitted to Japan by way of China.

175. *Manjuraku:* a dance of Indian origin said to have been transmitted to Japan by the priest Buttetsu.

176. *Ryo-o.* (See also Plate 8 and commentary and Plates 43 and 101.)

177. Child dancer's version of *Ryo-o.* (See preceding plate.)

178. *Konju.* (See also Plate 11 and commentary.)

179. *Bato.* (See also Plates 1 and 36 and commentaries.)

180. *Hokuteiraku:* a dance composed

by Emperor Uda (reigned 887–97).

181. *Dagyuraku.* (See also Plate 74.)

182. *Ama.* (See also Plate 109.)

183. *Kanshu:* a dance performed by either four or six dancers.

184. *Shunteika.* (See also Plate 102).

185. *Sanju:* a warrior dance. (See also Plate 62.)

186. Child dancer's version of *Genjoraku.* (See also Plate 100 and commentary.)

187. *Saisoro.* (See also Plate 39 and commentary.)

188–199. Dance poses demonstrated by Togi Hiroshi, member of the imperial Gagaku troupe.

188. The dancer stands erect, with both hands clenched and held at the waist.

189. The right arm and the left foot are extended forward, while the left hand remains at the waist.

190. The right arm swings to the side, and the weight is shifted to the extended left foot.

191. The first two fingers of each hand are extended, and the hands are raised above the shoulders, with elbows bent. The knees are also bent.

192. The hands are clenched and held above the head, while the left foot is extended forward.

193. The first two fingers of each

hand are extended, and the hands point toward the floor. The right foot is extended forward.

194. The right hand is extended to the left at waist level, while the left arm is extended to the side at shoulder level. Both hands are clenched.

195. The weight is shifted to the left foot, with the left knee bent. The first two fingers of each hand are extended. The right arm is extended backward at shoulder level, and the left arm is curved around to the right, also at shoulder level.

196. The left hand, with fingers curled, is held at the waist, while the right hand grasps the trouser leg. The right foot is extended forward, with the toes touching the floor.

197. The dancer kneels with head bowed. The right arm is extended to the side at shoulder level, and the left arm is curved around in front of the head. Both hands are clenched.

198. Opening pose of the Bugaku dance *Sanju.* (See also Plate 185.)

199. The left foot is raised and the right arm extended upward in a "left dance" pose.

200–219. Paintings of Bugaku performers in dances of the right. Owned by the Department of Music, Imperial Household Agency, Tokyo.

200. *Embu:* a congratulatory halberd dance performed by one dancer

of the right (shown here) and one dancer of the left. (See also Plates 103 and 170.)

201. *Shokuha.*

202. *Ayagiri.* (See also Plate 108).

203. *Komaboko.* (See also Plates 76 and 110.)

204. *Kitoku.* (See also Plate 40 and commentary.)

205. *Soriko.* This is one of the dances in which the *zomen* (general-purpose mask) shown in Plate 41 is used.

206. *Shimmaka.*

207. *Taisotoku.*

208. *Kotokuraku.* (See also Plates 42 and 99.)

209. *Nasori.* (See also Plate 3 and commentary.)

210. *Chikyu.*

211. *Shinsotoku.*

212. *Shintoriso.*

213. *Kocho:* a dance in the *dobu* (child dance) classification composed by Fujiwara Tadafusa in the early tenth century.

214. *Ringa.*

215. *Hohin.*

216. *Hassen.* (See also Plate 35 and commentary and Plate 105.)

217. Child dancer's version of *Rakuson.*

218. *Onin.*

219. *Ikkyoku.*

220. *Azuma asobi:* a native Japanese style of dance. (See also Plates 80 and 107.)

The "weathermark"
identifies this book as having been
planned, designed, and produced at
John Weatherhill, Inc.
7–6–13 Roppongi, Minato-ku, Tokyo 106
Book design and typography by Ronald V. Bell
Layout of photographs by Tanko-sha, Kyoto
Composition by Samhwa Printing Co., Ltd., Seoul
Color and gravure plates engraved and printed by
Dai Nippon Printing Co., Ltd., Tokyo
Text printed by Kinmei Printing Co., Ltd., Tokyo
Binding by Okamoto Binderies, Tokyo
Set in 11-point Monotype Baskerville
with hand-set Bulmer for display